Vodafear

An analysis of
Mrs. Best's
"Vodafone Values"

Volume 1 of the "Understanding Business" Series.

By J. Nason
BACentre

ISBN   978-1-84728-434-1

Preamble

A long while ago, I was in a place called Shanghai. I was seventeen years old, and devoted to adventure. We had sailed up the Yangtse accompanied by armed Chinese guards. I had a great interest in politics in those days.

A long while ago, I was in a small port in the Philippines. I was eighteen years old, and devoted to adventure. A man came up to me who was just as intelligent as me and no doubt far more moral. He asked `one piece bread`. It took me a while to understand that he was begging.

A long while ago, I was in a place called Hong Kong. I was seventeen years old and devoted to adventure. In the hold of a ship I saw an old woman who from endless years of backbreaking toil was permanently bent double.

A short time ago I was in a market town in England. It was prosperous, and I never met such fear.

Introduction

What follows is an account of some most astonishing events that occurred before and after the then `head` of a Vodafone department was sentenced to imprisonment.

It has been written, and the website www.vodafear.com, exists only because Mr. Chris Gent and Mr. Paul Wybrow have been unable to answer the very simplest of questions. Over a long time, many opportunities have been presented to resolve this privately, without response.

The central character suffered from an acute mental disorder. Perhaps we may agree to simply call it psychosis (although it was more than that), and we will refer to this person as `the Psychotic`. This person, for reasons which will be explained, had no realistic ability to control his actions. Those around him had every ability.

The surnames of the good people have been changed or removed, as they may not want to be associated with this, or may still work for Vodafone. The other names remain unchanged.

I/me

This account is written in the first person, because that is the only way it can be recounted. The I`s and me`s are otherwise irrelevant. I hope that in reading this, you may be able to put yourself in the place of the narrator. You will find that there are many things said about the I/me narrator, all of which, good or bad, have no validity or value.

This account does not claim to achieve any form of literary merit. Some of the text, particularly that from the original website, is emotional, or obscure, but that it is the way it was written at the time, and has been kept here. What is for certain, is that this account is accurate.

The purpose ? One time in an office in Newbury, the narrator said to the `Director of Human Resources` "No person, particularly no young person, should ever walk into something like that".

Your views: this account seeks to present an accurate record, but of course there are many ways to interpret the truth. It is hoped that you may present you views via the website, so that we may form a collective conclusion.

Yours sincerely,
JN

Chapter 1 Background - the origins of Vodafear

What most clearly needs to be conveyed is the history, structure and culture of the organisation called `Vodafone`, because unless you were actually there, it is difficult to believe such events could have occurred. I do not know whether this report is capable of adequate illustration, but we must hope that the subsequent sections will provide a basic illustration that you will find valid, and upon which you may make your own deductions. At this stage we may simply summarise.

`Vodafone` - literally Voice (from the Latin) + misspelled `fone` (phone). Voicefone. With the advent of mobile telephony in the 1980's, two companies were empowered by the government of the day. One was the vast bureaucracy of British Telecom, the incumbent telephone provider, and the other was called Racal, essentially a `defence` industry organisation with close ties to government. (In the world of that time `Defence` industry was, by the way, more generally associated with the business of killing people.)

Racal begat Racal Vodafone begat Vodafone (Voicefone).

The key to understanding all of the events that follow, is the organisational and social structure that was imposed at the beginning of Vodafone. The structures actually date from at least as far back as the Industrial Revolution. Despite the social advancements since that time, the fundamental elements of social control remained intact at the end of the twentieth century in a small market town in southern England.

The first real 'head' of Vodafone was a man called Gerald Whent. An article in a business newspaper was very perceptive and very accurate. It noted that Gerald Whent was not really interested in mobile phones, or communications, but was most concerned with power. In the greatest boom industry of that time, the phenomenal growth of mobile telephony, there was power. In one building there was a computer system that continuously recorded new connections to the network, the total relayed to Gerald Whent at regular intervals. A few years later, at an Annual General Meeting, a man named Mclaurin stared at a video screen that evidenced that Vodafone were involved in the communications of over one hundred million people. Power.

As a more practical illustration, Vodafone was described as the offspring of a nineteenth century manufacturing factory, and a quasi-governmental bureaucracy of a defence industry supplier. There was an extreme regime of hierarchies and levels, fear and obedience. I had thought the area where I worked to be the very worst but perhaps not. A man from one of Vodafone`s suppliers much later described to me the department with which he had to negotiate. He roared with laughter, and said "do you know, all the desks were lined up facing the front, where the manager sat surveying them. They were not allowed to talk to each other, unless it was concerned with the work in hand! "When I first joined Vodafone, I was informed that although the lunch hour was anytime between 12 o'clock and 2pm, nobody went to lunch before 12.30, and nobody returned after 1.29pm. Some years later, a woman said that she had recently joined Vodafone. "They said to me" we never go to lunch until 12.30 "...

What must also be made clear is that 'Vodafone' did not sell phones. Or fones. It simply owned the network licence. The legislation of the day, in an attempt to avoid concentration of power, insisted that neither the incumbent British Telecom or Racal Vodafone, could sell products or services to the public. Instead this was to be undertaken by independent "Service Providers'. No matter. From this central network licence, a small number of middle-aged white males in Vodafone discovered they had won every lottery.

Enough of this boring detail. It is necessary to provide a brief illustration of the central 'departments', and then we may get on with the real story.

The `Business Systems` department of Vodafone was part of a larger department called `Commercial Services`, an unusual choice of label for a department that had no sense of commerce and prided itself on not providing services. It was essentially an `I.T.` department concerned mainly with ancient and antiquated Billing Systems. All attempts at change, enhancement, or new products had to go through the `Business Systems` department. This was ideal, as in place as `head` of the Business Systems department was the Psychotic who had the most terrible fears, and was completely dependable to be totally obedient. Commercial Services could therefore use Business Systems to ensure that anything they did not want to do, fell at the first hurdle.

The `Business Systems` department was further logically part of the central Vodafone organisation. It was supposed to be responsible for the design and implementation of all of Vodafone`s new products and services, working with all other Vodafone areas, from the Network designers to Accountants to Service Providers , to ensure a successful and efficient development.. It was though unfortunately owned by 'Commercial Services' who had a vested interest in ensuring that as little as possible actually got approved.

Of the other departments, I discovered that everybody had a hatred of `Marketing` (except the humans who were categorised in that `department` of course.)

I soon learned that everybody really, really hated a division called 'Vodata'. Forget Marketing, Vodata were the real enemies. Out of curiosity, I tried to discover why everybody hated Vodata. The reasons seemed to range from they were political opportunists, to the bizarre fact that they didn't actually own the text messaging platform. Never mind, let's hate them.

All of this was overshadowed by a hatred of 'Service Providers' (the retailers). These were organisations that would defraud Vodafone at every opportunity, and were beneath contempt. I found this particularly strange, as these were the organisations that actually did the real work.

Far, far too late of course I came to understand that if you added all this hatred together, multiplied it by infinity and added a bit, you may get a pathetic underestimate of the hatred directed at those few humans who were categorised as belonging to a tiny department called 'Business Systems'. And the sources of this were the attributes of cowards and the attributes, operations and behaviour of the Psychotic.

Place all this in a small market town, where there was little alternative employment, with different 'departments' that hated each other in different buildings, and you may see the environment that supported the events of this history.

I've never believed in 'departments'. And, for example, if you took the trouble to compare departmental hatred, and say good old racial hatred, you would discover that there is no difference

Chapter 2 The beginning of the madness.

When, as an old man, I applied for the job with Vodafone's `Business Systems` department in 1996, an initial phone interview was set up. I received a call from a fine young lady, Jo, who asked me general questions in a professional manner

Before the following face-to-face interview, I received some words of advice from the agency about the Psychotic : "If he says `Which do you think is more important, written or oral communications, say `written communications`"

At the interview there were two other people. One was a woman called Jane Boiston from a department that was labelled `Personnel`, who was completely silent until the very end. The other was the Psychotic.

The Psychotic asked strange, meaningless questions, until finally "Which do you think is more important, written or oral communications ?" "Both are important" I replied.

At the end, Jane Boiston, who had sat silently for at least half an hour, asked one question. It was a question that held the key to one very important aspect of the Psychotic, although she did not know this.

What I was later to discover was that between the time of Jo`s phone call to me and the interview, the Psychotic and his friend, the devious and perfectly useless Mr. Paul Wybrow had ensured Jo's departure from Vodafone. Jo had gone to see  the very same Jane Boiston of `Personnel` in confidence, in an attempt to communicate the harm the Psychotic caused. Before she got back to the office, Jane Boiston had phoned the Psychotic to warn him. You may wonder, like many others, how anyone could do such a thing, but hopefully the true role of Vodafone`s `Personnel` department may be illustrated in what follows.

The Psychotic lied, blamed, and ranted in his madness, and went to see his friend Paul Wybrow. Paul Wybrow did grinning and shaking his head, and between them they got rid of the fine young lady called Jo. Once Jo had left in tears on Friday evening, the Psychotic realised that he could do anything he wanted to, and there was nothing anybody could do to prevent it.

I got the job. In hindsight, I really got Jo's job. From the agency the night before I started, I received a phone call : "A word of advice, just keep your head down".

Almost exactly one year later, a woman named Alison Stanton of the department `Personnel` gave me her absolute word, three times, that nobody else would be involved in my attempts to get the Psychotic to see the harm he caused other people. A few hours later of course she completely broke her word, when told to do so by Mr. Paul Wybrow. And Mr Paul Wybrow, said "would you say you`ve lost communication with the Psychotic", and then did grinning and shaking his head in the triumph of his deceit.

The first part of this report details the quite extraordinary events of that year. The second part of this report details the methods used by Vodafone to suppress all discussion.

Chapter 3 Travelling the world.

It was very cold when I joined `Vodafone` The air was cold, and I entered a silent cubicled office in a drab office building on a business park in Newbury. The Psychotic eventually came up to me and said in a strange voice, "Jo left to travel the world !" and went away again.

There was silence and an air of great anger in the cubicled office. I did not see the Psychotic for three days. The next time I saw him, he came up to me and said "Jo left to travel the world !" and went away again.

I began to ask the others if they had any idea of what I was supposed to be doing, as I had only been reading odd, meaningless manuals.

Twice in the next few days, the Psychotic came up to me and said "Jo left to travel the world !" and went away again.

Eventually, I understood, just, from the Psychotic that there were projects concerning a division called `Vodata` that should be taken over from a fine young woman named Vanessa. One day, I went to see Vodata with Vanessa, who was attractive, professional, hard-working and very, very angry. On the way back, she told me in bitterness of the nightmare that was the department called `Business Systems` in Vodafone.

I said stupidly, "I`ve just joined, so I cannot comment"

Vanessa slammed the door of her car so hard it would have registered high on the Richter scale.

"You`ll learn, you`ll learn!" she shouted in her personal despair.

On one of my first days, I listened to an exchange between the Psychotic and Vanessa , one of just three people left in the Business Systems department. In a weird voice, the Psychotic was desperately shouting "You should be more proactive, you should be more proactive!" Vanessa said desperately "Nicki Hodgson`s not inviting me to any meetings". "You should phone her up each day and see what meetings she`s got" shouted the Psychotic.

Six months before I joined, a woman named Nicki Hodgson had left the department, promising to take people with her, and set up office just down the road to re-start the same 'Business Systems' department under a different label, 'Marketing Development' She did not take the people with her of course, for reasons that will be explained.

And so I commenced on some 'Vodata' projects. I picked up three projects that were concerned with what was then called SMS, which is now more commonly known as text messaging. In those days, little use could be seen for this function, as it merely replicated the function of a pager - Vodafone already had a 'paging' division. I read through the many complex documents, attempting to discover what had been designed, or what had already been agreed. From the documents history, it was clear that many `business analysts` had been involved over time, then each disappeared from the next revisions. I was to much later discover that this was common to many of the projects. The cycle of professional people unknowingly joining the Business Systems department, discovering the madness, and leaving either by choice or by the actions of the Psychotic, had been going on for an eternity.

I do not wish to bore you with office details. Simply, there were monthly meetings at which projects were submitted for approval. Before this could happen, all of the Vodafone `departments` - Commercial Services (Billing), Finance, Marketing, Fraud, Legal and Regulatory, and many others - all had to have read the documents produced by 'Business Systems' and approved them. This could take endless revisions before a total agreement could be reached, and endless negotiations between departments that hated each other. There was enormous pressure for each project to be submitted for the next monthly meeting, at which projects were normally rejected anyway, just for the hell of it.

I took the text messaging projects, and in the first week I worked night and day to get them into some form of order. At the weekend I took the project documents home, and worked all weekend. By a deadline on Monday morning I had got the design documents in a reasonable shape. I had a quiet desk in the silence, by a window. I was aware of somebody behind me. It was the Psychotic. I turned, and the Psychotic asked me what I had been doing, in a strange, detached manner. I replied that I had got the text messaging design documents into an acceptable form. It was as though a switch was turned on inside the Psychotic. The hatred in the face was both astonishing and shocking. Up to that point, the only conversation or interaction I had had with the Psychotic, had been the bizarre interview, and his repeated assertions that Jo had 'left to travel the world'. And now in front of me, was a human being who evidenced the very extremes of hatred. There followed many supposed questions that had no sense, and I stood there in complete puzzlement. At each attempt to get back to a rational discussion, the suppressed violence, the hatred, and the absurdity become ever more intense.

I must provide a brief physical description of the Psychotic. I hope that you will not think that the following is derisory, because it plays a very important role in our collective understanding. Each of us is the product of our inheritance, our perceptions, and the immensely minor differences upon which we place such ridiculous and meaningless importance in our brief existence.

The Psychotic was short in stature, bearded, with a slightly hooked nose, resembling nothing so much as a disturbed garden gnome. If we may examine those attributes further. The perception of height among humans is most strange. For some reason some people completely devalue themselves because on a planet of many thousands of miles diameter, the top of their head may be a few inches below that which they have been conditioned to see as ideal. Ridiculous. The human perception of physical beauty is equally absurd, with the most minute differences in construction determining popular beauty or non-beauty. And most importantly, our co-existence is based on the very finest of balances of perception of reality. With the very gentlest of persuasions we may tip that balance into insanity.

And so, in a small 'Voicefone' office in a small market town, the Psychotic crouched forward in contorted hatred, a stream of violent voices emanating from the beard. Just as suddenly, the fit ended, and I was faced with a child with a strange ingratiating, pathetic look, silently shaking his head from side to side. This was the 'head' of Vodafone's central Business Systems department.

Chapter 4   Dignity for sale.

The `Business Systems` department was supposed to be the central function gathering requirements for all new services for the rapidly expanding Vodafone, documenting and designing solutions, and co-ordinating with all the `departments` . In all other mobile telecommunications companies this department would have been anything from twenty to fifty people strong. At the time of my joining, Vodafone's Business Systems department had three people, or four if you counted the fine young woman working on Satellite systems.

At some time later in this account, I must remember to tell you about an event that occurred a few months before my arrival. The four professional people worked from early morning to late evening, took work home with them, and worked most weekends. The Psychotic had stood in the middle of the office, and in a fit had repeatedly shouted at those four professional people " Work harder ! Work harder! .. or you will lose your jobs. Work harder ! Work harder! .. or you will lose your jobs. Work harder ! Work harder! .. or you will lose your jobs....". This was two months after Ms. Nicki Hodgson had left to start up the department under a different name.

These four people were Vanessa, of slamming the car door fame, an intelligent and angry man called Mac, a very fine man called Robert who helped everybody and whose designs made Vodafone literally hundreds of millions of pounds, and the young satellite lady of great wit and intelligence. Within two months, Vanessa and Mac would leave, like so many others, in despair.

But help was at hand.

Enter stage left, Mr. Marcus Cox. Who needs a chapter all to himself. Next Chapter.

We worked in one room, with the Psychotic occupying a closed office in the corner that resembled a Corporation Tip.   There were also two secretaries. One was the secretary of the Psychotic, a small and mousey woman who most enjoyed the reflected power. The other was a young lady of about eighteen years old, who had more humanity and commonsense than the rest of Vodafone put together.

This group of people, categorised and labelled as "Business Systems", were within a greater group called "Commercial Services". The head of this was a man called Paul Sayers, who's office was just down the corridor. It is not possible to describe how really scary this man was. Scary, scary, scary. He never talked to anyone, to upset this man was the end of your Vodafone career. His office deliberately overlooked the building entrance one floor below. Each morning he would look out of his office. Nobody ever arrived after 8.30 am. Scary, Scary, scary. Each lunch time he would look out of his office to ensure that nobody left before 12.30 and nobody returned after 1.29. Oh my, so scary. Return at 1.32 and you were unemployed. Nobody left before 5.15pm Monday to Thursdays, or 4.15 on Friday. Nineteenth Century factory hours.

Scary Paul Sayers had the next level in the hierarchy beneath him. One was the Psychotic, who was employed because of his extreme psychotic fears. The next was a man called John Tingey who most enjoyed threatening people, particularly women with young children. They are very vulnerable, and an easy target. He also spent much of his time trying to catch people out on expenses. Once he caught out a man who had inadvertently left a sixty pence bottle of water on a hotel bill. No drinks were allowed, and the man's career was in jeopardy. Once much later, I offered John Tingey a free email address I'd set up for him, obedience.dog@vodafear.com but never heard anything further.

The last of these was a man called Niall Garrett. Niall specialised in finding reasons for not doing anything. He was reasonably good at this, his lack of intelligence, imagination, creativity, or any sense of the beauty of our world equipping him well for the task.

The evolution of these structures was quite natural. The mobile phone industry was in a period of phenomenal growth, and further competitors had come into the U.K. market. Vodafone was run on fear and obedience, with a blame culture that pervaded every aspect of working life. Most changes to services meant changes to the Billing of services, and the Billing department ("Commercial Services") run by the very scary Paul Sayers used systems that were out-of-date and badly designed. It was therefore essential that whenever they were asked to do something that they could not achieve, they could destroy any requirements documentation and deflect any blame away from themselves. Having the Psychotic heading the business systems function was just perfect, with his fear and obedience to the 'department' unchanging and unchangeable.

If I may, I will give some simple examples here, and others later in the chronological order to which they belong.

One morning, I sat in the cold silent office, next to the fine man called Robert who helped everybody and was the designer of services that have since made Vodafone vast fortunes. The previous evening he had worked until 2am, and arrived in the office this morning before the legal deadline of 8.30 am. At around 9am, a raging John Tingey came straight into the office.(It was a measure of the relationship that he took no notice of the Psychotic who was nominally head of that department.)

He went over to the fine man, bent forward until his mouth was inches away from the fine man's ear, and repeatedly shouted "What did you tell them ? ! What did you tell them ?! He feared that 'Commercial Services' may be blamed for their inabilities, but then he had many layered fears.

I looked at this in disbelief. From later correspondence you may discover that I thought this one of the most cowardly and offensive scenes I had ever witnessed in an office. I looked around the silent room, where others stared at their screens. In the corner office, the Psychotic was slightly behind the door, witnessing this. He was both fearful and in awe.

Another early example involved myself. Among many projects, I had one that had an extreme deadline. That week, with two very good people from the 'Vodata' department, a solution using the existing functionality of the Billing system was defined and agreed. Late on Friday, everything was completed, and the design documentation updated late into the night.

On Monday morning we held a meeting to confirm to all involved that we had success. Mr. Niall Garrett then announced that the Billing department had now decided not to implement it in that way, and that an alternative solution would have to be sought with MIS (or M.I.S. – of this later). There was a silence in the room. All the work had been wasted. Being relatively new to Vodafone, what really shocked me was the air of triumph in the manner in which Mr. Garrett announced this. He seemed to think it funny that all of the Business Systems documentation would have to be re-done. I thought we were all supposed to be on the same side.

The people who dreamed up the new services were called "Marketing", and these mostly went though a department called "Marketing Development". This department was headed by the woman called Nicki Hodgson. The same Nicki Hodgson who, in her hatred of the Psychotic, had left the Business Systems department and essentially started the same function under a different name. To attain the ascendancy over the Psychotic's department, it was therefore essential that she build up her own department and ensure the increasing irrelevance of Business Systems. In other words, she had a vested interest in causing harm to the few people she had so recently worked with,

Everything was departments and sides, all of whom worked in different buildings in the small market town, and all of whom hated each other. On one side for example was the 'Marketing Development' department, on another the Commercial Services Department. And of course, being cowards, they did not address their concerns to each other, but fought their battles through the tiny Business Systems department who produced the designs. John Tingey would say about a project for example "Is this one of Nicki's. Is this one of Nicki's ?". You might think it much easier for him to phone her up and ask her, but that was not the correct protocol. Nicki Hodgson would say dismissively, "That John Tingey always thinks he's right". In the middle was the Psychotic who had such a terrible fear of all of them, and they used his fear without conscience for their own ends.

On other sides were Finance who hated Marketing, Service Providers (Retailers) who everybody despised, Vodata and lots of other units beginning with Vod who were unprincipled opportunists, Fraud and Security, Network Engineering, Customer Care and a billion other 'departments'. The basic job of Business Systems was to bring all of these into harmonious accord. Or at least try.

So for a few chapters now come to work in our tiny Business Systems department. As you will discover, the work you will do will have nothing to do with what was described to you at your interview. You will never escape the department, because all applications must go through the Psychotic, and he has such a fear of anybody leaving that department and staying within Vodafone, because of what they might tell others. And if you choose to leave, any suggestion of external comment will be met with the understanding that your 'reference' will not endear you to your next employment.

Welcome to Vodafone, leave your dignity at the door.

Chapter 5. I've been having complaints.

Drive to a pre-fabricated office building in a gloomy business park on the outskirts of a small market town. Park your car in the main car park. Do not park in a marked space. Marked spaces of ground are a reward for obedience and available only to those who conform.

Ensure you can reach the entrance way by 8.29 and fifty-seconds at the very latest. 8.30 and one second is a punishable crime. Walk up a metal stairway, turn right at the top on the first floor. Go to an office at the end of the building. Sit down at your desk. On your desk is an out-dated personal computer and a landline phone, your means of communication with the outside world. Decide to say good morning to the good people, Good mornings back then silence. Silence and anger. The fine woman Jo who went to Personnel in confidence has just been got rid of by the Psychotic and his friend the grinning Paul Wybrow. The Psychotic has approached you several times to say "Jo left to travel the world". Some months previously a woman called Nicki Hodgson had left and set up a rival 'department'. Endless people had come and gone from the department. But nobody tells you this. In the silence of the empire of fear, nobody says a word, and so you are completely unknowing.

Look as the Psychotic shouts "You should be more proactive, find out what meetings Nicki's got", ands from your desk, silently observe the despair in the face of the fine woman. Watch as John Tingey walks into a fine man's space and has `one of his little turns` as he himself described his repugnant sickness. Wonder what you are doing here, how you got here, and how human beings can possibly choose to live like this.

When your computer has started up, open your emails of conflict. Already you have more projects than would be allocated to five people in any other telecommunications company. Know that you will have to work until midnight again. Think that if you just walked out, how would you find further employment. You need the money, you have responsibilities. Look around the office.

On second thoughts, I think you should leave now, before you have images you will carry for the rest of your life, so I will revert to the I/me. I would invite you to one of our team meetings, but you would really not want to go there. Don't worry, you'll get another job, something will come along.

The first team meeting I went to was about a week after I arrived at Vodafone. We congregated in a small office. The Psychotic commenced the meeting with a hatred in his face, and the statement " Right, I've been having complaints about this department".   Over the course of the ensuing year, I suppose I must have gone to maybe thirty 'team meetings'. All but two of them commenced with the statement "Right, I've been having complaints about this department". They were not complaints about the department of course, but the conflicts that others inflicted upon the fearful Psychotic. And he then translated them into "complaints about the department".

The fine woman Vanessa worked non-stop, with great precision, and had done so for more than two and a half years.. At the second or third meeting, after the usual statement she said to the Psychotic in anger and despair "why don't you stand up for us, why don't you just stand up for us." The Psychotic had a strange grin, and shaking his head from side to side said "I do stand up for this department, I do". Nobody more consistently and deliberately betrayed the people he worked with than the Psychotic. People who worked fourteen-hour days, people who tried to help him. Because he had such a fear of the people around him. If you deliberately had to choose the worst place in the world for the Psychotic to be, at the nerve centre of the Empire of Fear would be the winner by a country mile.

The first team meetings at which I was present, were attended by the Psychotic, the mousey secretary to the Psychotic who enjoyed the reflected power, the fine woman Vanessa, a man called Mac who was doing tariff work, Robert who designed everything and helped everybody, Fenella who was mostly concerned with satellites, the narrator of this (I/me), and Marcus Cox. Oh dear, Marcus Cox. Marcus needs a chapter to himself. Next chapter.

After the complaints tradition, the objective was for each person to go through the projects on which they were working. These were exercises in pure conflict. As each person tried to explain what they were doing, they would be met with completely irrational comments from the Psychotic, who understood nothing about the work. There was the constant pressure of unrealistic deadlines and ridiculous workloads, and constant surreal aggression from the Psychotic.

I think it was at the third team meeting that I first realised that I was quite literally working in a madhouse. I looked at the Psychotic and wondered how on earth he had attained the position of 'head' of Vodafone's Business Systems department. I was later told that he had joined Vodafone as a contractor, with the very scary Paul Sayers, also a contractor. This was in the relatively early days of Vodafone. Both of them had decided to become 'permanent' employees. Paul Sayers somehow managed to become head of "Commercial Services", don't ask me how, and the Psychotic worked for him as head of 'Business Systems'. Later many people would say to me "How on earth did the

Psychotic keep his job, surely somebody would have done something. But the Psychotic was perfect for what Paul Sayers wanted, and he was fully supported by Vodafone's 'Personnel' department, and of course by the devious, grinning and perfectly useless Paul Wybrow.

One day I learned that Vanessa had decided to leave, although I am sure she did not want to. For two and a half years she had worked and worked and worked, but could not stand the despair any more. On her last afternoon the Psychotic decided to make a speech to the room announcing her departure. He seemed excited. Vanessa said a few sentences. At one point she showed a moment of weakness, and said bitterly to the Psychotic " why did you never let me work on the projects I wanted to ?" It was only a moment of weakness, for she was a strong young woman, but all of that despair had to have some outlet. When she was gone, the Psychotic had a quite open air of triumph. He repeatedly claimed that she obviously could not cope with pressure.

Shortly thereafter the man called Mac told me that he was leaving. I asked if he had a new contract. He replied not, but he would rather lose everything than work a moment longer there. He gave me many examples. He had some time ago resorted to writing down everything the Psychotic said. When the Psychotic then denied saying those things, Mac would present him with the written evidence. The Psychotic would shake his head in absolute certainty, and confirm he had never said them. One morning I witnessed an exchange between them. The Psychotic announced to Mac that a crucial meeting he should be at, had started an hour ago. Mac looked at him in disbelief. "Why didn't you tell me for God's sake" he exploded. The Psychotic just stood there grinning and shaking his head. After Mac left, the Psychotic repeatedly claimed that because of his work, Mac had very nearly closed the department.

I will mention one further happening that is related. One evening I was working late at the office, before copying documents to a disk to take home to continue working. There was nobody else in the office except myself and the Psychotic. Just as he was leaving, he came over, yet again with a look of surreal hatred. He slammed down a piece of paper on my desk and disappeared. I picked the paper up. It detailed that I was to give a presentation to the heads of various departments on the developments in text messaging. The time of the presentation was effectively the next working morning at 9am. I looked at it in disbelief. The Psychotic had deliberately left it until the very last moment to ensure that I would fail. I worked until about 3am. The presentation was accepted. Except for one person. John Tingey deliberately raised a minor point that nobody had identified, and nobody cared about. Back in the office the Psychotic was beside himself with stress about whether we could resolve the issue. I wrote two lines to resolve it.

So, within my first three months two more people left the department, effectively leaving Robert, Fenella and myself as the complete Vodafone Business Systems team. For all of Vodafone's new products and services. One day Robert went to the Psychotic and stated that as he was working 14-hour days seven days a week, he simply had to let some projects slip. In response the Psychotic assigned him two further projects.

All of these events follow a quite understandable and predictable pattern, and have a common causality. And they all actually concern Mr. Marcus Cox.

I will bore you with two more illustrations of the constant all-invading fear. One day I drove to Birmingham and back for a meeting with a bank. A couple of days later, discussing this, the Psychotic was suddenly gripped with the most terrible fear. "You can't claim expenses, you can't claim expenses if you didn't fill the form in before the journey" I said I was not interested in reclaiming a few pounds for all that bother, but it did not relieve his fear. "It's in the cookbook, it's in the cookbook" he shouted.

I asked Robert what on earth was this cookbook. Robert smiled and said it was a 'departmental manual' that the Psychotic had put together, and then laughing told me where to find it. I looked though this bizarre document, which ran to no more than five pages. In it was an odd collection of meaningless text that had been cut and pasted from some other documents, and bore no particular relevance to anything. On one page there was a picture of what looked like a water-cooler. There was of course no mention of expenses, cars, or anything else of any use.

And finally, the Psychotic once had a V.A.T. Inspector identify that on the shared department mobile phone there was a personal call included in a list of business calls, for which VAT (of about seven pence) had been reclaimed. Which is why thereafter the central Business Systems department did not have a Vodafone mobile phone on which to test or display or demonstrate any new service. Further Vodafone did not believe in providing staff with any discounts on mobile phones. They should be grateful to receive a salary. Which is why, like many others, I spent my entire time at Vodafone in Newbury with my trusty Orange phone.

Chapter 6 Communicable Diseases

Just when things could not possibly get worse, they got very much worse. One morning the Psychotic announced that there was going to be a change in the organisation structure. There was going to be a new 'team leader'. The responsibilities of this new team leader appeared to be exactly the same as those Marcus Cox was supposed to have responsibility for. Though, maybe this would give Marcus more time for giggling.

One morning a man appeared in the office. He was a reasonably pleasant looking man, prematurely grey, of slight build. One of his first actions was to slam the drawer of the photocopy machine with considerable force.

His name was Peter Chapman. He had just been thrown out of the Commercial Services department, and the one place they could dump him, was of course in the Psychotic's Business Systems department. I later learned that he had actually applied for a position in Business Systems a couple of years previously, and had been turned down because of his `attitude problem`. The Psychotic who had psychotic fits in the middle of the office and destroyed people's lives had decided Mr. Chapman had an attitude problem.

Why fate so set out to ensure I would never survive in that place I do not know, but it's next act was to position Mr. Chapman at the desk next to mine. I could listen to the heavy breathing of his anger while I stared out of the window in disbelief.

I will not detail the filth that he brought to those around him, it is far too embarrassing. Let's fast forward a couple of months, when we have discovered a little more about him. He had worked in the department run by Niall Garrett within Commercial Services. I began to discover that his knowledge of Vodafone was quite extraordinary, not just in the Billing section in which he had worked, but for so much else of the business. He must have had quite a thirst for knowledge and a need to create something worthwhile. Which is essentially why he was thrown out – this is not a joke, it is a fundamental element in the structure of that organisation.

If you will forgive my pathetic attempts, where people utter sounds that are not words, I will try to represent them in some way, such as the desperate exhales of Mr. Chapman's dejection.

One day he said "nhuh, I got fed up with finding reasons for not doing anything,"

The very scary Paul Sayer's structures were designed to protect 'the department' from any blame, and to deflect all work which may implicate the poor design of their systems. Niall Garrett was primarily employed to find reasons for not doing anything, something he could do quite happily until the end of time. In the purity of his racism, Mr. Garrett found it very funny that Mr. Chapman had been dumped on Business Systems. More of Mr. Garrett later.

Peter Chapman had announced when he arrived, that he "had not come to produce documents". If he was not going to do that, I had no idea what he was going to do. However, for one major project he was commandeered to write the feasibility study. Up to that time feasibility studies had essentially been worthless high-level drivel proving that any new service would make millions.

I read the first draft of Mr. Chapman's Feasibility Study for the major project. It was a work of very considerable accomplishment, and one that could only have been produced by someone with his depth and breadth of knowledge. For years he had rotted away in Commercial Services, working in a department run by brainless obedience dogs in an empire of fear.

One day Mr. Chapman said "Nhuh, I don't understand it. He (Niall Garrett) is alright out of the office. But in the office he's such a *w?nker*." For a man of considerable intelligence, Mr. Chapman should have understood the reasons for this. We'll educate him later.

One day Mr. Chapman watched John Tingey having one 'of his little turns, ironically with Niall Garrett. Mr. Chapman said of Mr. Garrett in disgust "He'll learn, he'll learn" Mr. Tingey did so enjoy stealing other people's dignity, perhaps because he had none himself.

But even more telling, one day Mr. Chapman spoke of a meeting he had been to. Obviously one of the people there who had not one hundredth of his knowledge had made offensive and disparaging remarks to him. (This man's name was also Peter but I do not have his surname) This was quite encouraged in Vodafone's hierarchies and much imitated by those who gained pleasure from such actions. Peter Chapman said "I went back in there after the meeting and said to him "that was out of order", and he said yes he was sorry" Over the course of the next months, Peter Chapman recounted this story at least five or six times.

The filth of his existence in Commercial Services was a disease which had entered his bloodstream, his brain and his soul. One time long ago, I sailed on a ship with a Chinese man who had no flesh. The ravages of drugs had rendered him to be a walking skeleton, the eyes blank and uncaring. I thought of this man whenever I looked at Mr. Chapman. The means by which Mr. Chapman assuaged the ravishes of this disease was to transmit it to those human beings around him. In the hierarchies and levels and caste systems of Vodafone there were rules governing to whom he could transmit his disease and to whom he could not.

He spent his days transmitting filth. Once I gave an example to a woman called Alison Stanton. It was so offensive that she gave an involuntary giggle. When he talked of the offensiveness he had endured for the sixth time, he had no realisation that he had become more diseased than those who had passed their disease to him.

Every time somebody returned his filth, he would say "Nhuh, it wasn't meant like that".

If I had said to Personnel "I sit next to a man who has contracted Diptheria. Diphtheria is an acute infectious disease caused by the bacterium Corynebacteria diphtheriae affecting the upper respiratory tract and occasionally the skin. It is characterised by an inflammatory exudate, which forms a greyish membrane in the respiratory tract. Virulent strains of C. diphtheriae produce a toxin, which can damage heart and nervous tissues. " even the useless Personnel may have decided to provide some help. If I said to Personnel, I sit next to a man who has a much more virulent disease and is constantly trying to damage the heart and nervous tissues of those around him, and if I gave them an example of his disease, they would giggle.

One time when I went to France I asked Mr.Chapman if he'd like some cheap tobacco. This act of kindness completely bewildered him, but he said yes. When on Monday I placed the packets of tobacco on his desk he looked like a beaten dog that does not trust what is being put in front of him, but at least he thanked me. The next day he went back to transmitting his filth.

One time he printed out a document, gave it to me, and said "have a look at this". It was a design document, from a bank of all places, written by a woman. I started to read it. The more I read it, the more I became engrossed. It was a beautifully written design, starting at a simple level, and gradually guiding the reader evolving into the complex solution that was proposed. It was a work of technical and literary brilliance, and that really is no exaggeration.

After an hour, I handed it back to Mr. Chapman. "That's what it's all about. Isn't it?" he said quietly.

Mr. Chapman designed the new processes for how the work of the Business Systems should be organised. It was excellent. The Psychotic stole it, put his name on it, and declared it to be his own work. Peter Chapman said – "Nhuh! I don't mind if he steals it, as long as it gets published." He did mind of course.

There is one final matter concerning Mr. Chapman about which I, nor anybody else, can offer any explanation. About six or seven times a day his wife would phone him. He was always angry, asking why she had phoned, and was completely dismissive. We gained from him an idea that his wife suffered from some disorder. These multiple phone calls happened every day without fail. One day he said to me "she is so fat". I had a vision of a beached whale.

Much later, after my departure from Vodafone, I saw him standing happily with his wife in a checkout queue at a supermarket. His wife was not only slim, but a most attractive woman. I phoned a fine man sometime later who knew him and said that could not possibly have been his wife. The man said yes she was, she was a fine woman. Inexplicable.

Chapter 7 Enhancements. A Classic.

My initial encounter with Mr. Niall Garrett was when he sent back his first review of my first document. As you may remember, it was a text messaging design which I had had to work on sixteen hours a day including weekends. Mr. Garrett rejected the document, partially on the grounds that MIS had been spelled incorrectly. It should be M.I.S. (the abbreviation for Management Information Systems.) At first I thought this was a huge joke, but on speaking to the few good people of Business Systems, I discovered that this really what was he was employed for.

Every time a new or amended service was required, Business Systems wrote the requirements and design documents, and had to distribute them to the entirety of Vodafone for review. Nothing could progress until all departments had approved the documents. Mr. Garrett was responsible for approving on behalf of Commercial Services. On behalf of the very scary Paul Sayers, Mr. Garrett's duty was to ensure that nothing got approved that Commercial Services didn't want to get approved. So for every document distributed, Mr. Garrett would search for spelling mistakes or missing items, and in the triumph of his detection, would always copy the scary Paul Sayers in his rejections.

Peter Chapman, who had accurately described him as a complete w?nker, said "I wouldn't mind, but he cannot send an email out without at least two spelling mistakes in it." This was perfectly true. The man who searched for the most minor error in every document sent emails that were full of mistakes. There must be a medical or psychiatric term for this.

At review meetings, Niall Garrett would similarly endeavour to reduce all discussion to the most extreme trivia, and each person in Business Systems would quote latest examples of his pedantry to the laughter of their colleagues.

There are therefore hundreds of examples, but there is one that rose above all others, and one for which Mr. Garrett became famous in many telecommunications companies.

The very fine man called Robert, who designed everything and helped everybody, was the designer of Vodafone's, and probably Europe's, first Pre-Pay system for mobile phones. It is difficult to remember a time when there were no pre-pay phones, and the concept was quite radical. This man worked night and day, and produced the first definition (I actually helped him on some aspects, and for some weeks we had a friendly rivalry as to who had worked the longest hours – 1,2 or 3am in the morning was not unusual). The document ran to over ninety pages, and covered every aspect from network design to top-up in shops, from banking partner interfaces to voucher codes. It was the basic service design which would shortly make Vodafone vast fortunes out of pre-pay phones.

As usual, it had to be distributed to every part of Vodafone.

One quiet afternoon, Robert called out to the office "Come and look at this, it's Niall Garrett's response." And so we gathered round his terminal., Fenella, Marcus, Peter Chapman, myself and a new young man of great ability and great humour.

Robert revealed Niall Garrett's responses. It read :

"On page 36 you have missed the d off of enhance. This proves to me this document has not been reviewed."

There were exclamations of disbelief, much laughter, and re-reading. There was nothing else just this sentence, and confirmation of rejection.

The new man said "Change it to denhance and send it back !". General collapse into roaring laughter. Brilliant.

Sometimes in two sentences you may see the complete man. Can you imagine Niall Garrett reading and re-reading this document, poring over every word, his finger moving slowly along each line of ninety pages. Can you imagine his dismay, when he could find nothing wrong, nothing to report to the scary Paul Sayers. Then finally there it was – on page 36 the word enhance had apparently lost it's final d. Elation, excitement. And then he sent the email, copied to Paul Sayers, proud of his achievement. Oh look sir, please sir, I've found something wrong again.

I witnessed a strange scene. One afternoon, there were a small group of people from other departments, who were discussing a subject in disbelief. It was the subject that for his services, Paul Sayers had promoted Niall Garrett to a Senior Management position. They stood there in disbelief and I stood there in puzzlement. They could not believe that such a w?nker as Mr. Garrett could possibly be so promoted. I was puzzled, because they all knew him and knew the Commercial Services, and should have realised that he was just what Paul Sayers was looking for. With John Tingey, Niall Garrett, and the Psychotic, he had a complete set.

Our brief lives are started and completed in such a few seconds, and what we do and achieve in this time is the measure of our brief presence. At this time, there were young people discovering new frontiers in many fields of human endeavour, arts, sciences, exploration, human understanding.

In a small market town a man wrote ""On page 36 you have missed the d off of enhance. This proves to me this document has not been reviewed.", and this was the value of his life. For this he was paid electric money. At the end of each month, Vodafone would present him with a statement of electric money which he could exchange for the endeavours and creations of other human beings. For the woman bent double and the beggar, just one month would be riches beyond imagination. Such are the values of our world.

I have a strange image of Mr. Garrett as an old man, tending his perfect front garden. Two young boys are roaring down the street, pretending to aeroplane pilots. Mr Garrett calls them over. "Do you want an exciting story" he asks them They nod yes. "Well, I was very senior in a large utility company in the billing department. One day they tried to build something, but I was very important and I inspected everything. Do you know what ? I discovered a missing d on page 36. Think what could have happened. The company rewarded me of course." The boys look on in awe. They move on, not pilots any more.

Chapter 8 You become what you hate.

Nicki Hodsgson was a wide woman with a slight lisp and an absolute hatred of the Psychotic. She had worked in the Business Systems department for some while. Well, to say she 'worked' in the department may be a bit of an exaggeration. On all of the documents there would be endless names of the business analysts who had worked on the requirements and designs, all of whom had since left in disbelief and despair at the madness.

One name that never appeared on any of the documents was that of Nicki Hodgson. Peter Chapman said "when she was in Business Systems she could start a Feasibility study, but that was about it." Another fine man said "she was always at meetings, so she never had time to actually do anything. She would come back, then give some information to one of her colleagues so they had to do the work."

I was an old man when I joined Vodafone, but until that point I had never worked in a large bureaucracy. I did work a long time ago for a hugely growing computer company, but that was in days of invention and excitement when there were no rules.

And so in Vodafone, I gradually came to understand some of the fundamentals of such organisations. Long ago, in a novel called Catch 22, there was a man who had "all the technical skills that would keep him poor forever". In Vodafone, to be someone who actually created something, was to be on a lowly path, of low caste. To rise in caste it was necessary to be in charge of the people who actually created value. To be in charge of people who created value, it was greatly advantageous to have no creative ability. The process is quite natural – if you cannot design a solution, bureaucracies will offer you paths to management. Or manidgment. Nobody understood this better than the Psychotic.

Six months before I had the misfortune to join Vodafone, Nicki Hodgson had left the Business Systems department to set up the "Marketing Development" department. On her departure she had said of the Psychotic "don't believe anything he says", and had promised that she would ensure the other people she worked with could transfer to "Marketing Development". She did not of course keep this promise. Far from it.

There were now two departments both of which were intended to fulfil the same function. One headed by Nicki Hodgson. One headed by the Psychotic.

In all of the conflicts and inter-departmental wars on "methodology", at various times the Psychotic would go to the Marketing Development department, and return saying "I've spoken to Nicki, I've spoken to Nicki !" Nobody had the heart to tell him that 'Nicki' was of course not only not listening or agreeing, but devoted in her hatred to his downfall. And the Psychotic would stand in the middle of the room shouting "The methodology ! The Methodology"

I first met Nicki Hodgson on one particular project, where she was having some difficulty with the Finance department. Being a soft touch, I proposed a solution and said to her "Do you want to propose this to them, or shall I". She stood there. "No, no you tell them" she said. She was of course quite incapable of doing this herself. When I went to Finance, an obnoxious little worm evidenced that he would not consider any more marketing projects as they were a complete mess " and you can tell that to Marketing Development!" It never ceased to amaze me how many times there were people in that empire of fear who were unable to simply sit down and define simple solutions, and instead of talking directly, would find intermediaries to carry their messages of conflict and inter-departmental hate.

I worked with two people in particular from Nicki Hodgson's "Marketing Development" department. The first was a very fine young man. He had recently left University, and was engaged on a major project. He had a natural talent, and a confidence to take on anything, One time I remarked on this young person's abilities to Nicki Hodgson. You could hear the fear in her voice as she said "He's just a graduate trainee, he's just a graduate trainee." She was of course quite unable to do any of the work that he had undertaken, but then she was a Manager. Or manidger.

The second was an extremely nasty piece of work called Paul Kerridge. There was a project called "Golden or Chosen Numbers". Good God. This was concerned with charging wholesalers and retail Customers more money for memorable or chosen numbers. Exciting. The charming Mr. Kerridge had been working on this for months. As he did not seem to be getting anywhere, I seemed to have got volunteered to help him.

The first time I met him, he sneered "I've been told I have to work with you, but I don't want to." He then went on to denigrate the people who worked for Business Systems. As he had never met any of them, I found his views particularly repugnant.

I asked for a copy of the design document he had produced, and when it finally arrived, it was obvious Mr. Kerridge had little idea of what he was doing. Which is why after months the project had not got anywhere. I arranged to get a workshop together with all of the Vodafone departments involved, and started to make some headway on re-starting the documentation. Mr. Kerridge refused to attend the workshop, saying he knew what he was doing.

Finally I managed to get him to a meeting with three key people. All four of us did our best to help him, as we went through his document. He was extremely nervous and aggressive, and at each stage shouted, "if you can't do it, strike it out !", Each one of us tried to explain that what we simply wanted was a clear indication of his requirements, then we would see what was possible. Half way through, Mr. Kerridge in his confusion demanded that all sorts of things "be struck out". That just about got rid of three quarter of the expected revenue. The people I was with were experts in their fields, and attempting to help Mr. Kerridge in his difficulties.

Suddenly Paul Kerridge announced to us all "you're only doing this because I'm a foreigner.!" We sat dumbfounded. What ? *What ?* Mr. Kerridge was from New Zealand. There was a long silence then we resumed.

Back in the Business Systems office I recounted this, and there was a discussion on why inverse racism was just as bad as the standard variety. Paul Kerridge had really tried to blame his ineptitude on the fact that we were against him because he was a `foreigner`. We also worked with two other fine people from New Zealand, and Paul Kerridge's remarks puzzled and offended them just as much. Mr. Kerridge by now had a reputation among many departments as an extremely unpleasant person.

Why fate did what it did next I shall never know. A man with great humour, after lunch, came back with a Kiwi fruit, placed it on my desk, and continuing the disgust of inverse-racism laughed "This is Mr. Kerridge. He's going to get us". There was laughter from the office, but if I'd known the future implications perhaps I would not have joined in the laughter.

As Mr. Kerridge refused to attend further meetings, I told him he'd have to distribute his document to the wider Vodafone community. The comments that came back explained carefully to him the options and the decisions that must be made, the inconsistencies and inaccuracies in his work.

I went down to Marketing Development to discuss these with him. As we went through each person's comments, Mr. Kerridge would make disparaging and offensive remarks about them. When finally he insulted a fine woman who was universally highly regarded, I closed my book.

Mr. Kerridge then said desperately "I asked you to get a meeting together!". I looked at him. For weeks we had been trying to get him to a meeting. He was fiddling with his desk, and suddenly one of the drawers fell out. I turned and walked out, behind me the man was now asking me to return. I'd had enough of trying to help him and kept going.

Back at the office I recounted this. Other people from Business systems recounted how they'd been getting complaints about him from many quarters. I wrote a brief summary of events, and copied both Nicki Hodgson and the Psychotic.

Some time later, the Psychotic appeared and stated he was going to see Nicki Hodgson to resolve this. He had that familiar and dreadful far-away dreamlook, matched to an air of triumph.

When he returned, he stood in the office and said excitedly "I've seen Nicki. I told her Paul Kerridge would make a very good business analyst, I told her that !"

There was as you may imagine a silence of utter disbelief. Through all of his psychosis, all of his clinical depression, all of his madness, the Psychotic must have sensed this, because he looked puzzled at people, looked from one to the other trying to understand the anger in their faces.

The Psychotic thought he might steal Mr. Kerridge from her.

Mr. Kerridge was the same stature as the Psychotic, had the same first name, and you could smell the same fear. He had phoned up Vodafone to ask for a job. Can you imagine when Nicki Hodgson interviewed him ? There before her was the winner of the Psychotic look-alike competition. She could not fail to employ him, despite the fact that he lied about his past experience.

I wrote to Nicki Hodgson but did not get the courtesy of a reply. So I phoned Nicki Hodgson. "What do you want to do.?" There was a long silence, the she said "this is for a Director, this is for a Director". I realised then that what happened in that department was that she got other people to do the work, then presented it to the higher levels in the Empire. It's called being a manager.

Nicki Hodgson wanted so much to destroy Business Systems, and now she was faced with the fact that Business Systems, in the shape of me, would have to take the project over. "I'll re-do the document" I said and put the phone down. Over the next week, working non-stop, I wrote a completely new document. As an old man, I knew these `golden numbers` had been around since the beginning of telephony. I started the introduction with this, illustrating with Whitehall 1212. You have to be old to know who's number that was.

In the middle of this, I went into the Psychotic's office, where he was sitting with Marcus Cox. "There have been so many complaints about Paul Kerridge, he's got no idea what he's doing, and you told Nicki Hodgson he'd make a good business analyst!" I uttered to him. The Psychotic shook his head in absolute certainty. "I never said that, I never said that" In the following team meeting, when Mr. Kerridge's name was mentioned, the Psychotic recalled how he'd had trouble with somebody and a friend had gone and knocked the man out. He would get in touch with this person, and get them to knock Paul Kerridge out." This was of course all pure fantasy.

At the next meeting, I turned up early at the meeting room. Paul Kerridge was alone, and was distributing copies of my document to the empty places. "It's much better than I could have done". This rather took me aback. I sat down in silence to await the others.

The Psychotic in his fear destroyed the lives of the people who worked in Business Systems. Nicki Hodgson in her hatred of the Psychotic, did her level best to bring down Business Systems. Each wanted and needed the ascendancy, the labels of self-worth. At one time the Psychotic said of her attempted takeover "She won't do it. She won't do it, she'll never get the funding!" In her hatred, Nicki Hodgson had become indistinguishable in her ambitions from the Psychotic. It is our human nature. We are attacked by terrorists and we are righteously out for revenge, whereby we ourselves become terrorists. We become what we hate.

A long time later I was walking with some fine people in the summer countryside. I suddenly blurted out a sentence to them. I had not thought about it, I had no idea I was going to say it, it must have been deep within my consciousness for a long time. It just came out. "If you ask me, the most evil one of the lot was Nicki Hodgson". I stood there astonished and embarrassed at myself. There was a silence. Then a fine man just said "Yes.", and everybody agreed. The word 'evil' is wrong of course, she was not evil. But she devoted much time and effort to harming the people from Business Systems. When she did not invite Vanessa to meetings, she knew what trouble this would cause. When the extremely unpleasant Paul Kerridge made disparaging comments about people he had never met, those views could only have come from her. And as we may see, when she was presented with people who tried to get Business Systems working properly, this was not at all to her liking. At the meeting with Alison Stanton after my departure, I informed her that Nicki Hodgson hated the Psychotic and had left the department to start up a new one to rival it. Mrs. Alison Stanton looked startled. We will never know what clever deceits the Psychotic used on Nicki Hodgson, but he so easily fooled her, just as he so cleverly made fools of many others.

Chapter 9   Ooooh, I know about Business Systems, me.....

Perhaps it is time to finally introduce Mr. Marcus Cox.

I had the misfortune to encounter `Vodafone` about one week before Mr. Marcus Cox joined. I first met him in a reception office. "What are you here for ?" I enquired politely.

"Ooh, I`m joining Business Systems. I know about Business Systems, me " replied Mr. Cox. Goodness me I thought, there`s a confident fellow, just what we need. "I`m working in that department as well" I volunteered. Hopefully we could work together to conquer the world, although he did seem just a little bit strange.

And so Mr. Marcus Cox was employed as the `Senior` Business Analyst in one of the world`s leading telecommunications companies. His job was, with his vast experience and skills, to manage and lead the department. Oh dear.

In the first month it was noted that Mr. Cox was a very conscientious worker. He turned up every day at eight o`clock,  some thirty minutes before the empire of fear`s official start time. He sat at his desk and diligently read Personal Computer magazines. Usually until about ten o'clock or ten-thirty. It was then time to chat to the secretaries. It was then time to chat to anybody else. Until the empire of fear`s official end time. Day after day.

By the second month, it was becoming apparent that Mr. Cox didn`t actually seem to do anything. There was beginning to be an eerie suspicion that perhaps Mr. Cox was not quite what he seemed. But we were constantly re-assured. By Mr. Cox himself.

Mr. Cox`s technique was to wander over on frequent occasions and for example tell stories of what had happened during his journey in. "Didn`t you see that accident" he would exclaim. "Oh dear, I don`t think I`d like to be a passenger in your car !", and he would do strange giggles. This carried on forever.

Nobody is quite sure when Mr. Cox first started work. There was a standing joke in the office that `Marcus joined Vodafone in February, and started work in August. Then stopped again in September." But let us give Marcus the benefit of the doubt, and say his first attempt was probably before August.

I believe that his first attempt was on an `Insurance` project. The first document that I or anybody else saw was a programming flow-chart.

What on earth this had to do with defining Insurance requirements, nobody was quite sure. Some time later `The Psychotic` announced that Marcus would not be working on the project any more. It hadn`t been quite what the customer was looking for.

I do not know what the next of Marcus`s projects was, except that he informed us "They`re saying it`s just two existing documents cut and pasted together. And it is !", and Mr. Cox did giggles.

At some stage in the proceedings, Mr. Cox came over and told me "The Psychotic says I`m not pulling my weight. And I`m not!" and Mr. Cox did giggles.

Mr. Cox became Mr. BluffBumble. The picture was of Mr. Bluffbumble on a high wire with a long pole. At any instant he must surely tumble to the ground. But he never did. Despite all the events that we thought must finally cause that last wobble and crash, Mr. Cox stayed on the high-wire. Because he had a guardian angel.

All of this was accompanied by the never-ending tales of his adventures and expertise, followed by derogatory remarks about other people. After a few months, we were growing somewhat tired of this, and I duly suggested he shut up. It seemed to break the spell. At least for a little while, Mr. Cox attempted some work.

I should at this stage confirm that nobody wished any harm to Mr. Cox, he had just become an irrelevance in the nightmare that was `Business Systems`. Mr. Cox walked back with us to the car park in the evenings, Mr. Cox might walk down the shops with us. And, as you may see, I once invited him into my home. And two fine people helped him greatly to survive in that nightmare.

Then came Mr. Cox`s greatest project. I am not sure quite what part of mediation or billing it was concerned with - as Mr. Cox`s view was that he was *the* designer of Vodafone`s new Billing system, perhaps it was all of it. Mr. Cox then sent out his document.

Quite proudly he showed me some of the comments. One man had written "This is the worst document I have ever seen." Another wrote, "After page 8, I gave up any further review." Mr. Cox said "I`m not going to let The Psychotic see these comments", and Mr. Cox did giggles.

There was one key event. Mr. Cox went to see Mr. Garrett. When he came back he said "When I went in there, Niall had written "CRAP" in big letters on the front of the document. I wasn`t going to let him upset me, so I carried on !", and Mr. Cox did giggles.

One time I went, with Mr. Cox, to visit a department with hundreds of systems. Almost as we were leaving, our guest showed us one particular system. Mr. Cox made some bizarre comments. I said to our guest "Is that a VB front-end ?", and it was confirmed so. Mr. Cox then made some further bizarre comments about `VB`. When we had left, and were out in the street, Mr. Cox said "Oooh, I`m sorry about what I said about the VB bit." He was rather red and shaking a bit. I thought no more about it until a few days later, Mr. Cox started offering to write a VB front-end for anybody that wanted one. These offers continued for some while. It was a standing joke in the office, that at the appropriate moment we should take Mr. Cox up on his offer. But the fine people in that nightmare had much greater concerns.

After many, many months, Marcus Cox didn`t seem to have actually achieved anything, and one afternoon, he was over with his bluff tales yet again. "How many projects have you actually got to the PAG Marcus ?" we asked. Marcus did giggles. As a very friendly joke, it was decided that Marcus was the Norway of the PAG projects. Marcus, nil points. Mr. Cox did giggles. The next morning, he came rushing over, red and giggling, and handed me a piece of paper. It was full of words such as `rape` and `shit`. I showed it to the fine man next to me. I read only the first couple of paragraphs of this filth, and said to Mr. Cox "Where on earth did you get this Marcus?". Mr. Cox did giggles, and said "ooh, um, it was going round where my wife works." I would place a very large wager that Mr. Cox received it in his previous employment.

One day, Marcus Cox came up to me and said "At my last job, a woman tried to have me fired because I didn`t do anything !", and of course he giggled. I said to a fine man in astonishment, "Why on earth would he actually tell me that." But it continued. One day Marcus Cox informed me `At a previous job, I was put in charge of a department of forty people. On my first day, they`d put a big sign over my door "This department run by a w??ker". One day, Marcus Cox informed me, "One time a Director said "What do you do Marcus". I replied. "I find out what people want" "And then what do you do Marcus ?"

You may indeed wonder why Mr. Marcus Cox would volunteer this information, but perhaps you may understand that he`d been carrying all this with him for a very long time, and at last in Vodafone, he found an environment where he could extract his revenge upon the world, and be protected and encouraged while he did it.

One fine day we got a project leader called Peter Chapman. He`d been told "there is a vacancy in the Business Systems department, and you will take it". He came with such filth, I could not possibly recount it..

The point is of course, that there was no such vacancy. Mr. Marcus Cox was employed as the `Senior` Business Analyst` in all of Vodafone to manage the department, and lead it heroically into a new dawn. But in the empire of fear, this did not matter, because what the empire of fear wanted was control and obedience and nothing else.

Once this `team leader` joined, Mr. Marcus Cox passed his days in learned discussion. At one time for about three days, he stood behind the `team leader`, making suggestions about `Project Manager Workbench`. Really, this went on for days. Mr. Cox`s contribution consisted solely of repeating what the team leader said, as sage advice. Finally, Mr Cox said "at my old place, we had someone to do this for us", and giggled.

And for a couple of days he earnestly discussed an entity relationship diagram with the `team leader`. This consisted of repeating `one to many` and `many to many`, after the `team leader`. If you had asked Mr. Cox what the point of an entity relationship diagram was, he would not of course have had the slightest idea. (although once this is published, he`ll probably rush out and buy a book on it.)

Throughout all this, Mr. Marcus Cox was regarded as a harmless and useless bluff merchant, and he continued to walk back in the evenings with us, and walk down to the shops with us. But in an empire of fear, such people are never harmless. Far from it.

Just when everybody though he must surely crash to the floor of the circus, yet again he was saved. `The Psychotic` decided that the very fine young lady, Fenella, would now work for him.

This fine young lady was duly instructed to work for Mr. Marcus Cox. Of course, the first thing Mr. Cox did was to assign to her all of the bizarre documents he`d managed to make some attempt on. And then of course, within a few weeks as `Senior` Business Analyst, started to tell outside departments "Oh of course, Fenella has not completed those documents yet." And did giggles.

The young lady had great character and challenged him saying "Marcus, have you been trying to blame these documents on me ? ". "Ooh no !", exclaimed Marcus Cox, and did giggling.

This young lady, like so many fine people before had no choice other than to leave, although of course she did not want to, and having great courage, went directly to another department. All such applications were supposed to go through the Psychotic, who in Vodafone terms was a `line manager`. And she succeeded.

The Psychotic at first went into a psychotic rage, for three reasons. Firstly, despite his irrational hatred of the people who worked there, he could not afford for it to be seen that yet another fine person was leaving. Secondly, this fine young woman had intelligently bypassed him. And thirdly, what the Psychotic could never afford was for somebody to leave the department and stay with Vodafone. Because of course he feared so much what they would recount.

Shortly before this, The Psychotic had been shouting at this young lady "Eight pages a day, eight pages a day!". He had of course a mad obsession with churning out as many `documents` as possible, with the idea that this would save him.

Then the Psychotic tried reasoning. "There will be training, there will be training!", he shouted in a desperate attempt to keep the fine young lady in the department.

The young lady did not of course really want to leave. But faced with the giggling Mr. Marcus Cox, and the Psychotic, there was little she could do.

At this time, a `man` called Mr. Wybrow came to be selected to be in charge of the Commercial Services department. The `team leader` Peter Chapman as usual foresaw this. He said "If Paul Wybrow can survive that, he can survive anything." It will be interesting to discover just what and how the devious, grinning and perfectly useless Mr. Wybrow survived in his previous position.

The Psychotic of course discussed the fine young lady with his friend Mr. Wybrow. And Mr. Wybrow, grinning and shaking his head, said to the fine young lady "Don`t worry, we`ll get you back", and the fine young lady left.

And of course, Mr. Marcus Cox went to tell stories to the people in this fine young lady`s new department before she joined. What Mr. Marcus Cox in his fear did, was to wait outside the office each lunchtime, and waited for the person who the fine young woman was going to work for. And when this man passed by, Marcus Cox would accompany him each day to the shops. And do giggling.

At this time, I was concerned with `groups`, but I will not bore you with the details. I remarked that the concept of groups was fundamental to a project Mr. Marcus Cox was working on. Mr. Marcus Cox had produced some marvellous documentation on this project. It consisted of the same picture repeated but with different captions on `platforms`. Some while later, the `team leader` and myself went to see the Psychotic and Mr. Marcus Cox.

The Psychotic announced "Marcus cannot think of everything, his document is a view.". The `team leader` and I looked at this astonished and perplexed. A view ? What the ???? is a view ? ` The Psychotic announced again, that it was a `view`.

The Psychotic and Mr. Marcus Cox sat there together, huddled together for shelter from the world. One the head of Vodafone's central Business Systems Department, the other Vodafone's most Senior Business Analyst.

Chapter 10 Obedience Dog

For one year I worked in this environment. I had a great shame, and wondered what my family would possibly think if they saw me like this. If they really saw an old man in that place of obedience and fear. I used to sit there, staring out of the window, and remember freedom. I am sure you do not want to listen to much more of this, but with your agreement I'll just illustrate some further events before we come to the second part of this account.

On one of my first projects, I wrote a Business Requirements document which wasn't bad. Not wonderful, but not bad. One morning the Psychotic came over and said "John Tingey says you've saved this department. He says you've saved this department." I am not able to describe the mixture of the Psychotic's elation, and an underlying irrational hatred. The statement was ridiculous, but the Psychotic's fear of losing his department was very real.

One time, I went with the Psychotic to the office of an obedience dog called Mr. John Tingey. It concerned a major project in which, unfortunately, the Billing System were essential. There were a couple of other people at the meeting.

To my astonishment, John Tingey said he'd thought of a solution. "Tell me if I'm wrong, tell me if I'm wrong." I gawped. *What ?* For the first time in his life he was going to do something positive, something creative. This was against the law of Commercial Services. Most people at some time have a human need to produce something of worth before they shuffle off. It is a basic human instinct, the instinct that has provided all of the product, knowledge, and communication with which we now surround ourselves.

There was only one thing wrong with the solution, it was three months too late. During this review, John Tingey made several derogatory remarks about the Psychotic and his department. I looked at the Psychotic, slumped, fearful of this man. I stared at John Tingey and my attitude was plain for all to see. So Mr. John Tingey decided to have one of his turns. When he'd quite recovered, he said "when can I have this ?". I wondered what he was talking about. What he meant was he wanted Business Systems to document the solution. There were three reasons for this. The first was that he was incapable of documenting it himself. The second was that humans at his level in the caste system did not do documentation. The third was that if anything went wrong with the solution he could distance himself from it. That evening I worked until midnight documenting a solution I knew was three months too late.

When we got back to the office, the Psychotic sat slumped at his desk. He said bitterly, "some of those things John Tingey said were terrible". John Tingey continually goaded him, knowing his fear. I made a decision, as usual a terrible decision. I decided to try to get the Psychotic to stand on his feet. "How do I make a complaint about that disgusting sod ?" I asked. The Psychotic was immediately alert and quite excited. "You can go to Personnel" he said.

When I announced that I was going to Personnel, Peter Chapman said "nhuh, that's unfortunate, John Tingey thinks highly of you". I stared at him. Even the compliments were lies. "No of course he doesn't" I replied, "he denigrates everybody in this department and covers it with false statements."

And so I set up a meeting with Jane Boiston. The same Jane Boiston who had phoned the Psychotic to warn him of Jo's visit, although I did not learn this until much later. At the meeting I described to Jane Boiston how at every turn John Tingey did his best to denigrate or destroy the work of the Business Systems department. I'd had a number of personal examples which I recounted. Jane Boiston said sullenly, "are you sure you're not projecting this, and really it's the Psychotic who's the problem ?" I replied "him, no he wouldn't stand up for anybody. What can I do about John Tingey? " "You can escalate this, or arrange a meeting with John Tingey to review" Neither of these options had any value in the hierarchies of fear.

I had never visited a Personnel department before. I sat there, it all seemed so pathetic, people actually choosing to live like this. "I'll think about it " I said. When I got back to the office, the Psychotic ran up to me to ask how I'd got on. When I told him it was not worth escalating, he was so disappointed.

One time, in the street outside, John Tingey said "you two will be working until midnight again, all the work that the Psychotic's taking on. You'll be scribbling until midnight. None of this would happen if you worked for me." So that was what the career was. Scribbling. Degrees in Business Sciences, Computing, years of experience, to end up as a scribbler.

I also had no idea why anybody would want to work *for* a man who enjoyed threatening people, particularly women with young children. That's ridiculous, working *for* some other human being. We join together in companies to work *with* each other. We work *for* our families, ourselves, or whoever or whatever else we choose.

Unbelievably, a few days later, the Psychotic rushed over to me and said "John Tingey says he supports this department" I looked at him. "No of course he doesn't, he uses this department and our documents to control what happens," The Psychotic looked bewildered. Later that afternoon, he rushed over again "I've told John Tingey to stop using our department, I told him that". He stood there, a brave man. For the first time he'd really stood up to him. But of course it did not last, and within a short time he was in great fear of what might happen to him as a result of his bravery. I really should not have tried to get the Psychotic to stand on his feet, it was an action of my vanity that could have caused him more harm.

After about six months, the Psychotic requested I meet him in his office. As I went in, the look of hatred was again astonishing. In his hand he had a white envelope, crushed in the anger of his tight grasp. "This is for you!" he shouted. "I was the only one who lost money, only me" I had as usual no idea of what he was talking about. I managed to extract the envelope, and left the office. I announced to the others "I think I've just been fired". I opened the envelope. The letter began "thank you for all your hard work", and noted a 2% pay rise (an amount I later earned in a morning when I returned to contracting.) Robert said "Paul Sayers cut his raise by one half a percent for missing something " I would imagine that half per cent to be worth about one hundred and twenty pounds per year after tax. It was how Paul Sayers controlled the Psychotic. The previous year, Paul Sayers had given him a bigger salary raise, and the Psychotic had danced in the centre of the office repeatedly shouting "I run this department for me ! I run this department for me !"

I was in the Psychotic's office. I said to him "Who's department is this? Is it our department, or is it Paul Sayers, or is it John Tingey's, or is it Nicki Hodgson's? " Who's is it ? I thought his response would be a bitterness against Nicki Hodgson who had set up as his direct rival. "This is not John Tingey's department!" he kept repeating, and he was close to tears.

In small offices in a market town, human beings acted out their parts in insular, isolated, invidious departments.

For one project, I decided to become a revolutionary and arrange a workshop right at the beginning of a project to bring all these `departments` into one room, to try just for once to get them to work together, This sounds heroic, but I was only one of a number of people with this simple ambition, and the ambition was taken up by some good people from Marketing. The Psychotic asked if he could come to my meeting. I had a terrible desire to tell him to go away for fear that he would sabotage it, but in the event, it went well, and most people were pleased. It didn't change anything of course.

Later on another project, I was working on a major project that involved every Vodafone department, including unfortunately Billing within Commercial Services. There had been many meetings and workshops, and much difficulty in getting a solution from Billing. One morning, my desk phone rang. I picked it up, and an anonymous voice threatened "I've been asked to remind you which department you work for." In disbelief I just said "what?". The voice threatened again. "I've been asked to remind you which department you work for." I was about to answer "I know which ????ing department I work for, it's called Vodafone", when I recognised the voice as John Tingey's. There was a silence and the line went dead

Chapter 11 Christmas Greetings.

On December 24th. I received an obscene email from a young lady. You may think this a compliment for an old man. However the young lady sent it to hundreds of people, and she was in no way attractive. She was the secretary of Paul Sayers, and enjoyed the reflected power.

The email read "Sir Gerald Whent has decided that the offices will close at 3pm today. Therefore nobody will leave until 3pm." That was it, nothing else. The Christmas Greeting.

I was in an outer office of another department where this obscene email was being discussed. "This is like being in the army" I remarked. There was a fine young man there. "No it isn't Jerry" he said, "it's like being in school." The young man evidenced the natural disgust of all young people to the inherited stupidity of the "benign dictator".

Chapter 12 The suit.

It was announced that Gerry Whent was retiring and that he would be succeeded by a man called Christopher Gent. It was announced that Christopher Gent would visit the offices one afternoon.

At the appointed time, there was an order to assemble in the offices of MIS (or M.I.S., sorry). The door opened an in walked three grey men in suits. They stood there. In silence. Such was my luck that I was next to the Psychotic. He was gripped in the most incredible tightness, the veins standing out in his neck, slightly crouching. I have never actually seen someone with lockjaw, though I once had an aunt who apparently suffered from it. If I describe the Psychotic as having lockjaw, it is only a convenient description and not medically accurate. Perhaps you think I exaggerate such things for effect, but I would assure you that it was beyond my capabilities of description

Through the side of his mouth he was trying to say "do you know who that is, do you know who that is, it's Chris Gent !" Awe and adulation and dribble in the extreme.

The grey men stood there. The one called Chris Gent had an expensive pinstripe suit on. He did not say "Hello shipmates, partners and pals !" He did not say "Isn't this a great industry to be in, isn't this such an exciting time.!" He didn't say "My name is Chris Gent" He didn't say hello. He didn't say anything.

The three grey men left in silence, and the door closed.

The Psychotic had travelled a long way to find Vodafone. There he found his home. The hierarchies of obedience would protect him, the indoctrination gave him the self-worth he so desperately sought. The Psychotic said "I don't mind what I do, I don't mind what I do, as long as I can work at Vodafone !"

A few weeks later he entered the office, and I noticed he was wearing an expensive pinstripe suit.

Chapter 13 Manidged

"You won't get out of here. All applications for transfers have to go through the Psychotic " Only one person had ever really managed it, Nicki Hodgson. Fenella had bypassed it, but in the end it was the grinning Paul Wybrow who really effected her removal from Business Systems. Afterwards, Fenella said of Paul Wybrow in disgust, "I thought he was serious, but he was just devious."

And so I thought I would try an experiment. I had been working with a group called Vodac (dealing with corporate clients), and in the internal vacancies there arose a position for a Business Process Analyst with them. So I applied for the position. I completed the form, and duly gave it to the Psychotic. Later that afternoon, the Psychotic came over to my desk. He was waving the application in the air, and he had that strange smile. "Let me see", he said, "I think I know someone over there". He named a double-barrelled name. I later discovered that this person had joined at the same time as the Psychotic. He seemed quite triumphant. "They've got Business Process analysts there have they ?" He'd obviously got an idea.

I might mention here that at this time, with Nicki Hodgson attempting to takeover the department, and the Psychotic declaring that the nasty piece of work called Paul Kerridge would make a good "Business Analyst" , I decided to ask the Psychotic what was meant by the title "Business Analyst", what skills did such a person need to possess, what work did they do ? I was in his office. "What kind of Business Analysts work here ? " I asked him. He looked blank. "O.k., is this a business analyst quite like an economist looking at macro business strategy ? " He looked blank. " Is this business analyst like working for a broker analysing company financial information ? " He looked blank. "Is this business analyst like an I.T. systems analyst must know C++ ? " He looked blank. There was a silence. "Why don't you just employ technical authors " I asked. I must apologise to all of the world's technical authors. Their profession is an extremely skilled one, but it has almost nothing to do with Business Analysis. The Psychotic thought about, and nodded. He had no idea what a Business Analyst was and no idea of the true role of a technical author. He was the head of Vodafone's business systems department.

I went for the interview. As I came out of the Business Systems office, I had to walk the length of the High Street. It was so strange, coming out of the madness back into a street full of people who smiled, talked to each other, laughed, and lived a life of freedom.

At the interview office, the man I had worked with and who would be at the interview smiled hello, and went into the office. I sat outside. For about twenty minutes. Finally I was asked to enter. In the office were the man I knew and a lady from 'Personnel' (later 'Human Resources'). At Vodafone, all job interviews required someone from Personnel to be present. The people from Personnel of course knew absolutely nothing about the work of any of the departments, and seemed to be there solely to ensure that the rules of social control would be obeyed. They really were an immensely strange group, who were there only for "senior" managers. They were much despised by everybody I worked with.

I looked at the woman from Personnel. She should have had a big neon sign over her head reading "You're not going to get this job". Goodness, the ill-disguised hostility in the look. The man I had worked with asked me sensible questions, I gave valid replies. The woman from Personnel was getting more and more uncomfortable. I was waiting for the moment. The man I had worked with gave information about his department. I agreed on basic principles. The woman from Personnel was getting quite agitated. I was waiting for the moment. The man I had worked with and I exchanged pleasantries. The woman from Personnel was about to explode. Here it comes I thought.

It was the woman from Personnel's turn.

"You know about eye tee, but what do you know about bisniss ?" she finally burst out. I did not quite know how to tell her that I first worked for my father's company when I was eight, had gone through every aspect of running companies by the time I was twenty-five, that I had degrees in Management Sciences and Business Administration, as well as years in `eye tee` as she pronounced it (Information Technology". But I knew this wasn't it. The real hostility was still there waiting. I gave a brief reply which she didn't listen to. She made a couple more comments. Then finally it arrived, what the entire interview had been working for.

"And how " she said.
Here it comes

"And how"

come on

"AND HOW DO YOU LIKE TO BE MANIDGED ?"

I think that is one of the most obscene sentences ever uttered by a human female. Later, I wondered whether Personnel and 'manidgers' held secret meetings. Perhaps every Monday night, if you hid in the shadows, you might see them furtively entering a dark entranceway. Women from Personnel, and John Tingey who liked threatening women with children, and the Psychotic who later announced "Women are no trouble if you hit them !!" and others. And when it was quiet, you could move to the door, and listen in. And you might hear the voice of a woman`s excitement "Manidge me !   Manidge me ! Oh, yes, yes,. manidge me more !"

"And how do you like to be manidged ?" In that one sentence you may see the complete woman.

I returned to the Business Systems office. The Psychotic had of course provided a terrible reference to Personnel, and no doubt included details of the complaint about John Tingey (about which he had been so excited). I went in to the Psychotic's office. He was grinning. "Why do you do this?" I asked him. He sat with that faraway look, grinning in triumph. "Why do you do this ?" I asked again. No reply, just the grin.

A couple of days later the Psychotic came over to my desk, a white envelope clenched in his hand. He stood at my desk, holding up the envelope as though playing some game. "This is for you" he finally said, grinning. It was of course a letter saying "on this occasion". That was the moment when I knew I had no future in that place.

I called the woman from Personnel and said I wanted thirty seconds of her time. Grudgingly she agreed. In her office I said "Can you tell me whether the Psychotic had any input to that interview ? "Ooh no, " she replied.

Later, after Vodafone, I asked Mrs. Alison Stanton for her name. "Was it, I think it was, erm, I think it may have been, now let me see .." She could not quite remember the name of a woman with whom she worked every day.

Later, after Vodafone, I asked Mrs. Pauline Best to confirm whether the Psychotic had any input to that interview. "I'm afraid that's confidential" was the reply. But then, everything was confidential as we shall see.

Immediately after my interview for a Process Analyst position, the Psychotic stopped shouting "The methodology! The methodology !" , and started shouting "The processes ! The processes !" One sight will stay with me forever. The giggling Marcus Cox, Vodafone's senior business analyst, occupied a cubicle next to the fine new man who had recently joined. The new man had written a design document of great merit, which believe it or not, had to be reviewed by Marcus Cox. One afternoon we stared at the sight of Marcus Cox standing up at the division between their cubicles. He was red faced, giggling, and almost sucking the top of the cubicle much as a baby does at the side of a cot, "I can't see the processes, I can't see the processes !" he kept repeating.

Immediately after my departure, the Psychotic and Paul Wybrow together changed the name of the "Business Systems" department to the "Business Process" department. And decided to employ technical authors. Oh dear.

Chapter 14 Do you want a drink ?

In the small market town at the end of the twentieth century, dignity was a scarce commodity. One fine man said to me " if this business was in London, half the people here would leave tomorrow". This was quite true. The combination of its location, the booming industry, and other factors served to effectively suppress the turnover. At one time, one major I.T. department had an annual turnover of 25%. One in four actually left, though nearer one in two would actually liked to have left each year. In other words within two years the equivalent of the entire department would have walked out.

I use to smoke in those days. I was outside with an excellent project manager. "Jerry", he said, " if you stay here you would get used to it". The next day I heard he had gone, gone to another mobile phone company, so he was given a month's money and told to leave immediately. He was very accurate. Living in an empire of hierarchies and fear, of levels and caste systems, with labels of self-importance so important, after a while you could get used to it. It would become the way of the world. Imagine if all of the world was that society, that children were born into it and would know no other.

There was an extremely pleasant woman who ran the department next door, who's name was Judy. One morning she was at my desk. I have elsewhere said she was close to tears, but I think that's an exaggeration, she was simply in a state of despair. "John Tingey phones me up anonymously each morning, and asks meaningless questions, just to check that I'm in. " She had three young children, and had asked Paul Sayers if she could arrive fifteen minutes late at 8.45 am so that she could take her children to school, and she would work half an hour longer in the evening. Paul Sayers had of course refused, and John Tingey then phoned her anonymously each morning. "What can I do, she continued, "we need the money and I can't get on a train to London each morning. I can't go to Personnel, nobody can."

I have theories about people who have children and those who do not, and I'm sure you don't want to hear them They are concerned with the proposition that there are men and women who do not physically produce children, but have children nevertheless, and there are men and women who have physically produced children, but do not have children. I'd better leave it to one of my external studies.

John Tingey could not possibly have had children. No man who has ever walked in the meadows with his children could ever bring himself to do as he did. Imagine each morning in the small market town, as these two people woke up. The fine woman would arise and have her family around her. Look at the clock, make sure you leave to always ensure your never arrive at work after 8.30am. Not for this woman the laughing, arguing, noisy , bundling into the car, or walking in the morning sunshine to school. She gets into her car and drives to the empire of fear. The man in another part of the market town gets into his car, driving to a different building close by. The woman gets out of her car and walks to her desk. The man gets out of his car, enjoying the anticipation of his first call. On the woman's desk, the phone rings.

This happened every day.

Meanwhile, in Business Systems, the Psychotic has such a fear and awe and despair of how this man treated him. And yet. John Tingey, having witnessed the nightmare of the people in Business Systems, said darkly "none of this would happen if you worked for me". He constantly goaded the Psychotic, playing on his fears. But somewhere underneath was some attempt to understand, some attempt to communicate. On one project, I had communicated with external Service Providers for the simple reason that the project could never succeed unless I did. I got a phone call from John Tingey. "Paul Sayers has banned all communications with Service Providers. If you carry on, you'll drop the Psychotic right in trouble. You wouldn't want to do that would you." This was said not in a threatening way, but in some form of concern for the Psychotic. I could hardly believe it, but tried to understand it.

To all concerned please excuse references to rats, this has nothing to do with anybody, particularly not the Psychotic, but simply as an allegory, I remembered a passage in a story by Lu Hsun in his Selected Stories. As this is in the public domain I have reproduced it below.

"Mei Chien Chih had no sooner lain down beside his mother than rats came out to gnaw the wooden lid of the pan. The sound got on his nerves. The soft hoots he gave had some effect at first, but presently the rats ignored him, crunching and munching as they pleased. He dared not make a loud noise to drive them away, for fear of waking his mother, so tired by her labours during the day that as soon as her head touched the pillow she had fallen asleep.

After a long time silence fell. He was dozing off when a sudden splash made him open his eyes with a start. He heard the rasping of claws against earthenware.

"Good! I hope you drown!" he thought gleefully and sat up quietly.

Getting out of bed, he picked his way by the light of the moon to the door. He groped for the fire stick behind it, lit a chip of pine wood and lighted up the water vat. Sure enough, a huge rat had fallen in. There was too little water inside for it to get out. It was just swimming round, scrabbling at the side of the vat.

"Serves you right!" the boy exulted. This was one of the creatures that kept him awake every night by gnawing the furniture. He stuck the torch into a small hole in the mud wall to gloat over the sight, till the creature's beady eyes revolted him and reaching for a dried reed he pushed it under the water. After a time he removed the reed and the rat, coming to the surface, went on swimming round and scrabbling at the side of the vat, but less powerfully than before. Its eyes were under water--all that could be seen was the red rip of a small pointed nose, snuffling desperately.

For some time he had had an aversion to red-nosed people. Yet now this small pointed red nose struck him as pathetic. He thrust his reed under the creature's belly. The rat clutched at it, and after catching its breath clambered upon it. But the sight of its whole body--sopping black fur, bloated belly, worm-like tail--struck him again as so revolting that he hastily shook the reed. The rat dropped back with a splash into the vat. Then he hit it several times over the head to make it sink.

Now the pine chip had been changed six times. The rat, exhausted, was floating submerged in the middle of the jar, from time to time straining slightly towards the surface. Once more the boy was seized with pity. He broke the reed in two and, with considerable difficulty, fished the creature up and put it on the floor. To begin with, it didn't budge; then it rook a breath; after a long time its feet twitched and it turned over, as if meaning to make off. This gave Mei Chien Chih a jolt. He raised his left foot instinctively and brought it heavily down. He heard a small cry. When he squatted down to look, there was blood on the rat's muzzle--it was probably dead.

He felt sorry again, as remorseful as if he had committed a crime. He squatted there, staring, unable to get up.

By this time his mother was awake.

"What are you doing, son?" she asked from the bed.

"A rat".

He rose hastily and turned to her answering briefly.

"I know it's a rat. But what are you doing? Killing it or saving it?"

59

I will try to complete this section with the minimum of further illustration, and then complete the second and final section describing how Vodafone suppressed all free speech and issued it's threats of corporate action.

In the last two months of my time in the empire of fear, the Psychotic was quite openly and obviously degenerating into complete breakdown. Despite this, absolutely nothing changed. Late one Friday afternoon, the phone rang. To my astonishment it was the extremely scary Paul Sayers, who never spoke to anyone. "How are you getting on, all the projects seem to come from you". "I'm just fine thanks" I lied, let's get this weird conversation over as soon as possible. " "Oh now, come on, " continued the extremely scary Paul Sayers. He then discussed the Psychotic, and Peter Chapman. . "I just want you to carry on for a few more weeks". I put the phone down, and just sat there. Paul Sayers knew all about the actions of the Psychotic, and just kept him there while endless good people came and left.

It was mid-afternoon, and the Psychotic emerged from his office. He had a document in his hand, which concerned a project I was working on. Somehow through his mouth he was saying something about John Tingey, something about trouble. Near to my desk, he was crouched forward in a psychotic fit. The muscles were strained, the veins standing out, the words meaningless. He was on the very edge of extreme violence.

"Don't go near him when he's like this". It was Peter Chapman. I realised later that Peter Chapman must have seen this before. I stood up next to the Psychotic, and told him gently that Marketing were still completing some work. "What's Marketing got to do with it ! What's Marketing got to do with it!" he kept emitting over and over. If you have never seen anybody in an extreme psychotic fit, it is beyond my capabilities to describe it to you.

By an astonishing coincidence, at that moment, the person from Marketing I had been dealing with walked in the room. And the switch clicked again. Immediately the words stopped, and the Psychotic looked at the person, and shaking his head and smiling the Psychotic said hello.

Nobody knew what the Psychotic did all day long. At certain times of the day he would emerge from the office and holding one arm in the air in triumph quote the share price.

He decided to review all documents. On one of mine he had written some changes on one page. There were six sentences, and numbers one, two, three five and six all began with "In addition". None of the sentences made any sense whatsoever.

Later, the giggling Marcus Cox emerged from the office saying "he's put yellow stickers everywhere". I went in to the office, where he had a document of mine. I sat down with him. On each page, he had put tiny pieces of post-it notes against sentences. As we went through the document, he would demand to know what something meant, or to say it was wrong, against each tiny yellow sticker. None of what he said had anything to do with the document. He was trying to move back into reality and failing. Suddenly he just stopped, and looked and said something about this was silly wasn't it ?

He had a fear of just about everything. Of John Tingey, of Paul Sayers, of Nicki Hodgson, of all the people who came to work in the department, of the V.A.T. man, of the time I parked in an empty manidgers car park, just everything I was discussing with a project manager the need for an audit trail in one particular project. The Psychotic was watching us, growing ever more fearful that there might be a wrong decision. The project manager finally agreed. The Psychotic jumped to his feet shouting "We need an audit trail, we need an audit trail!" I was discussing an issue with somebody else, and said "excuse me, I do not understand this, perhaps you could explain". The Psychotic looked on in disbelief. He could not believe that it was perfectly normal for an adult to say "I don't understand this", for adults to discuss and exchange knowledge.

By now, Niall Garret's brainless sabotage of everything Business Systems tried to do was far beyond any humour. Everybody in the department raised these issues at every team meeting. On one project, even John Tingey said with contempt and disdain "Niall will go through it with his fine-tooth comb as usual. Bless his little cotton socks" But the Psychotic had such fears. "I can't go to John Tingey with complaints about Niall Garrett unless I've got evidence. There should be a replies quality matrix in each document." And so he tried to get everybody to put a matrix in which would rate the quality of everybody's replies, a certain way to alienate absolutely everybody. The only purpose of this was to bring notice to John Tingey of complaints about Niall Garrett. Except of course that John Tingey, like everybody else, already knew everything there was to know about Mr. Garrett.

The new man who had started was a very fine man, of great ability and humour. He was quite tall, fine looking, and everybody liked him. Except from the moment he joined Vodafone, he had so many enemies. Niall Garrett sabotaged his work, John Tingey had his little turns, Marcus Cox giggled at him, and Peter Chapman distributed his diseases to him. Nicki Hodgson had a racial hatred of him, as she did for all people who continued to work in Business Systems. He was the most open and pleasant of people, and one afternoon he came into the office and said of Nicki Hodgson "I do not like that woman". Can you imagine her anger. More than a year earlier she had set up a department to take over the Psychotic's work, and here was an accomplished man who would continue to prevent this. I said to him "You must wonder just what you've walked into." He replied "I thought I was coming here to...." but did not finish the sentence.

The one with most fear of course was the Psychotic. Quite bizarrely, soon after the Psychotic and Marcus Cox had interviewed him and he had joined, there was yet another scene in the office. The Psychotic was standing right in front of the new man, looking up at him with such a hatred. He shouted meaningless questions, and at each attempt that the new man made at a sensible response, the Psychotic's anger grew, and the meaningless words increased.

The new man often made everybody laugh. After my departure, at a meeting of ex-business analysts, he recounted his interview, After the formal interview, the Psychotic had said he had to come for a drink. The giggling Marcus went along as well. At the public house, the Psychotic told him about how great a department was Business Systems, and how happy everybody was. He turned to Marcus Cox. "You can verify that, can't you Marcus ? " Marcus Cox giggled. "I can honestly say I've never enjoyed myself so much !"

Very near the end, I was working late. I became aware of somebody standing behind me. I turned, and it was the Psychotic. He was trying to say something. "What ?" I said. Several more times he mumbled incoherent words. Finally I understood, he was trying to say "Do you want to come for a drink". I sat looking at him. "Not right now, I've got too much work. Perhaps some other time."

For about eight or nine months I had worked literally non-stop, seven days a week, although I was not the hardest-working member in that `department`. Shortly before, Peter Chapman had come across to me and said sadly, "He said he didn`t know anything about it as it wasn`t on the timesheets." As usual I went over to his office, and he had as usual the air of triumph.

There was a very fine man who nobody will ever understand kept everything and everybody going. I had put some considerable effort into trying to get the Psychotic and the `department` to stand up, as many far better people had done before me. This was a very stupid thing to have done.

I said, with much bitterness, "that's the fifth or sixth time that disgusting little bastard has betrayed us. " This was irrational of me, as I knew of the Psychotic's illness and depression, but I must confess that I by then loathed the sight and sound of him so much, that I didn't want to understand. And I wrote a report on one year of madness at `Vodafone`, and did nothing with it, while last desperate attempts were made at any form of communication.

Chapter 15 Scared of you.

Paul Sayers was very very scary, probably one of the scariest people ever. Each morning he overlooked the entrance. He spoke to no-one.

A fine young woman said to me "My husband has worked in the same building as him for years, and he has never even once said good morning or hello."

Another fine young woman recounted how on a tour of the MIS (sorry M.I.S.) department, he had ordered the removal of a fridge. I know you don't believe me, but he really did. The people in that department were not of a sufficient status to have a fridge (even though they'd bought it between them.). They'd bought it so that they could put milk and food in it, including baby-food that they might buy during their lunch hour.

Mr. Sayers controlled the Psychotic, and used his fear.

To even look at Mr.Sayers in a wrong way was the end of your Vodafone career.

Among many other crimes in the Empire of Fear, I was guilty of the crime of looking. The first building I was in had narrow, metal-floored passageways. Many months into my time, I was walking round one corridor, when coming toward me were John Tingey, the man called Peter (who had so upset Peter Chapman) , and Paul Sayers. I could not help it. I just looked at them. I just looked and wondered where on earth they came from. My crimes were no doubt noted and filed.

One sunny afternoon, I found an excuse to visit one of the other offices, actually the head office although it was quite small. Leading up to the entrance were two paths, from either side of a small square. As I walked up one path, I looked up and saw Paul Sayers walking up the other path. The same Paul Sayers who had said over the phone "I just want you to hang on for a few more weeks."

Paul Sayers looked up and saw me. Immediately he did a strange shuffle-foot and avert eye routine, to ensure that he did not arrive at the entrance at the same time as me. He was of course scared of people.

Paul Sayers was a useless scared weak little weasel, who so lacked any self-confidence or natural ability, that he constructed his own sub-empire of fear within the outer one. And so the fear was layered, each level of the caste system fearful of the one above it, and controlling the next one down through fear.

What if senior, senior, senior management had discovered a fridge in an office of insufficient status. End of the world.

Paul Sayers was not scary, he was scared. Scared of me, scared of you.

Chapter 16   A love story

The fine young lady, Vanessa, who had slammed the car door, had said on her departure "this department won't be here in six months", and she was only a few months out.

Shortly before my departure, I went into the Psychotic's office, closed the door. The Psychotic looked dreadful, and was in some other world. I said "If you don't do something, if you just don't do something now, those people out there are going to lose their jobs."

He stared at me, swaying slightly. "It is all the fault of those people who went before, they didn't want to go to a low enough level. But it's going to be alright, it's going to be alright." He just sat there repeating this over and over and over and over. One time long ago I had a time of great pain that caused me to suffer from an illness called depression. It should not be called that, for it is a very serious illness caused by chemical imbalances.   In those days I used to do much exercise for sport. Returning from the gym and running track for example, I would park my car, then find myself unable to get out of the car. My brain would not command my body to get out. And so I sat there looking around where the houses and field and shops and everything else no longer seemed real. After some time I recovered with the help of fine people. It is not an uncommon illness, and I have been lucky enough never to return to it. And in this office, there in front of me was a man who was not only severely Psychotic and had been all of his life, but was further in a state of extreme clinical depression.

A meeting was arranged to try one last desperate attempt to define what the purpose of the department was. What came out from the fine people there was all of the professional experience that had been submerged for so long. The Psychotic as usual made strange and bizarre comments, but then he was descending into complete collapse. At one stage he told the fine new man that he did not understand the future of mobile telephony, it all depended on inter-carrier billing records. By this time, such deranged outpourings were so common that they were not in the least remarkable, now an accepted way of life.

At one stage The Psychotic said "Paul Sayers has offered me a job in charge of sixteen people, but it's not what I want to do". Paul Sayers, who had watched so many desperate people leave Business Systems, was now proposing to put him in charge of another department.

The Psychotic kept repeating "What I want to know is what's going to happen to me?".   It was only later of course that I realised the real significance of this sentence.

I was sitting beside Mr. Marcus Cox, who was red, and I could actually see him shaking. Because of course he understood nothing of that which the experienced and professional people were discussing. After about thirty minutes, in his fear, he blurted "What are we going to do now ?"

A short while after the meeting, a fine person came over to me and said in total disbelief "Do you know what The Psychotic said. Do you know what he actually said?"
He said "Marcus said "What are we going to do now ?" This proves to me he is Senior Manager material."

The Psychotic needed two senior managers and then he could move up to the next level in the hierarchy. He had destroyed so many people's working lives, until at last he found someone so weird, so useless, and so willing to participate in simulated activities, that at last, at last, he'd found someone he wasn't afraid of.

He only needed one more for a set. And he very nearly made it, as we will discover.

Pure and perfect lovers. It was a fine young person who first announced that Mr. Marcus Cox's middle name must surely be `Sucks`, although there was of course no actual sex involved. They had both commenced to imitate each other. They had both travelled so far and through so much to find each other, in `Vodafone`. I do not mean this in any derisory way, for each of us has our fears, our faults, our insecurities which we carry with us on our journeys. It really was a perfect love story, for two people to have so found each other and so needed each other.

It was a quite natural process of course. All of the Psychotics actions had been directed at achieving this. For each person who joined the Business Systems department, the Psychotic would immediately fear what they might think of him, what they might be told about him. So in his fear, he immediately set about destroying them. He ensured that the projects Vanessa wanted to work on were given to others. He deliberately sabotaged Mac's projects. He piled so much work on Robert in the hope that he would leave. For myself, giving me the presentation details at the very last moment was just one of many examples of how he attempted to destroy my work. And as each person left, he had a release of his fear, for he was burying the evidence and soon there would be no-one left who would be a perceived threat.

Near the end of my time, I invited Robert and Marcus Cox to my home for a glass of champagne to thank Robert for all of his help without which none of us would have survived. As I proposed the toast, Marcus looked a bit lost and puzzled.

Two postscripts. After my departure, Robert discovered that Mr. Marcus Cox had stolen his document, changed a few words, and put his own name on it instead. The man looked disbelievingly at him. "Why on earth did you do that ? " "It was crap" announced Mr. Marcus Cox, and giggled. You see, he had carried that day in Mr. Niall Garrett`s office for a long time.

A few months after my departure, and after The Psychotic`s imprisonment, I saw Mr. Marcus Cox. He sometimes passes my house on his way to work. The same house where a few months previously he had sipped champagne. He actually let me out into the traffic. Mr. Marcus Cox was sitting in his car, and was of course giggling. I said to Robert "I saw Marcus Cox today". Robert said "I wonder why he didn`t mention it."

After a suitable time, Mr. Marcus Cox was `promoted`, in return for services rendered.

Chapter 17   The price on the label.

The Psychotic and Paul Wybrow got rid of a fine young lady one week before I had the misfortune to meet Vodafone. A few weeks before my departure, the Psychotic and Mr. Wybrow arranged to get rid of another fine young lady. Mr. Wybrow did grinning and shaking his head, saying "don't worry, we'll get you back." Mr. Cox did giggles and following people.

One evening a few weeks before my departure, I sat down and wrote a report of one year of madness at `Vodafone`. Apart from one reference to Peter Chapman (and an understanding one at that), and one mention of a nasty little piece of work called Mr. Kerridge (who the Psychotic briefly tried to steal from Ms. Hodgson, then decided he would get a friend to knock him out) there is no mention of any person other than The Psychotic. When I read it, I wondered how on earth I had ever managed to survive more than a few weeks. It also mentions that I would never have survived more than a few weeks if it had not been for some very fine people in many `departments`.

Nothing was done with this report while last desperate attempts were made to get any form of communication with The Psychotic Apart from his severe psychotic disturbance, he was quite clearly suffering from clinical depression. In confidence, I asked two fine people to review it and tell me if it contained any inaccuracies. I said to them " you must not be involved. If you would just let me know if anything is incorrect I would appreciate it. Then you must forget you ever saw it."

We discussed what could be done with the report, for in the Empire of Fear there was nowhere to go. Paul Sayers knew everything that had gone on, and as a useless weak disgusting little weasel just continued his sub-empire of fear and protection. Everybody warned me not to go to Personnel, `they were only there for Senior Management and betrayed everybody else". I was given numerous examples. For some while we considered John Tingey. This may be surprising, but he had at least admitted that he knew how terrible the Business Systems department was, and on one occasion made some attempt to care or have an understanding about The Psychotic. But John Tingey would not have the power to do anything, even if he wanted to.

And so, I decided that I would have to go to Personnel, and discovered the new contact name was one Mrs. Alison Stanton. Don't do it Jerry.

Finally, at ten o'clock one morning I turned to Peter Chapman and said "it's no good, he's in there telling lies again." Peter Chapman just grunted. Lost somewhere deep under there was a real person.

I walked into the office of The Psychotic, and handed over the report in a sealed envelope. I learned fifteen minutes later that what he actually said after I exited was "Oh good, at last somebody is putting something in writing." About thirty minutes later, a raging madman almost ran over to me, and was shouting

"I want to discuss this in my office ! I want to discuss this in my office !"

I did, of course, have no idea that he was a few moments from going to prison, but I learned much later that one person at least, did. My `report` must have been one of the worst-timed ever in the history of the world. The Psychotics` rantings were a combination of madness and desperate pleas. I have often wondered what would have happened if I had discussed this in his office. I later became convinced that he would have divulged at least part of his nightmare.

I told The Psychotic that I would only discuss in confidence in front of an independent witness, Mrs. Alison Stanton of the `Personnel` department. I had been through many private meetings with The Psychotic, all of which made absolutely no difference, for a very good reason. The Psychotic refused to discuss the report with Mrs. Alison Stanton, and of course it was a few weeks later that I understood why.

"Come in Jerry"

"Hello Mrs. Stanton, thank you for seeing me". I had in my hand a sealed envelope with the report in it.

"What`s this about Jerry ?"

"Mrs. Stanton, this is very important. It concerns The Psychotic."

"Oh yes, what is it"

"I cannot hand this over unless you give me your word that nobody else will be involved. I don`t care what happens to me, but nobody else must be involved. It is very important".

"What is it ?"

"It`s a report on one year at Vodafone, but it`s about The Psychotic. It is very important that nobody else is involved. I am not going to hand this over unless you give me your word that this will be kept between us and The Psychotic.

"What do you want me to do ?"

"I want to discuss this report with you and The Psychotic"

"Yes that`s fine, I`ll see when I`m available`.

"Thank you Mrs. Stanton. It really is very important. You give me your assurance that nobody else will be involved ?"

"Yes, of course, Jerry".

I hesitated. Alison Stanton had agreed three times that nobody else would be involved. There are some actions that we take in our lives that we may regret for ever. If I had known what was to follow, I would never have uttered that phrase of false bravery "I don't care what happens to me" and I should never have handed over the envelope.

I handed Mrs. Alison Stanton the sealed envelope.

An appointment was made, and I walked back to the office, with the stupid belief that something vaguely intelligent might occur with regard to the madness.

The following memorandum duplicates much of what has already been written, but it is important to keep developments in chronological order, so you may just want to skip to the next Chapter.

The text of my report follows. This is what The Psychotic read in his room before he came raging out. When you read his response two hours later, you will see that his is a work of genius.

My Report.

INTERNAL MEMORANDUM

To:	Paul K	From:	Jerry N
cc	Alison Stanton	Date:	March 10, 1997

Re: Attached summary of first year in Vodafone.

Please let me have your written comments on the attached summary of my first year in Vodafone, with regard to any errors of fact or interpretation.

I will be seeing Alison Stanton on Thursday morning to discuss this further

J. Nason   Statement of Employment within Vodafone Business Systems
February 1996 to February 1997

I joined Vodafone Business Systems as a Business Analyst in February 1996.

For the first two weeks of my employment I did very little other than find manuals to read. I had no assigned tasks, and indeed The Psychotic hardly spoke to me during the first weeks of my employment. Towards the end of the second week, I asked other members of staff if they had any idea of what I was supposed to be doing.

During this time, I also became aware that there was extreme animosity between The Psychotic and members of the Business Systems department. The Psychotic in particular seemed to display an extreme animosity towards Vanessa , and Mac.

On the few occasions that The Psychotic did speak to me, he repeated that Jo had left the department to travel the world. It was only much later that I discovered that Jo and The Psychotic had not spoken to each other for months, and that The Psychotic had frequently reduced Jo to tears. Jo had taken her complaints to the Personnel department, and was then subject to extreme verbal abuse by The Psychotic for having done so.

In the third week of my employment, I learned from Vanessa that I was to take over certain Vodata projects from her (she had put considerable effort into these projects, and had wanted to see them through). At no time had The Psychotic advised me of this, or given me any information. I accompanied Vanessa to a Vodata meeting. On the way back, Vanessa told me that the department was a complete nightmare, and that The Psychotic was, to put it politely, disturbed. She further explained how I would discover, like everybody else who had ever worked in the department, just how awful it was. I replied to Vanessa that as I had only just joined, I could make no comment. As we left the car, Vanessa repeated to me "You'll learn, you'll learn.". Those were indeed prophetic words.

Without any information or advice from The Psychotic I commenced the Vodata projects. They were deemed very urgent, and I was required to meet extreme deadlines. The first weekend I took what documents I had home, and on my personal p.c. managed to complete the first BSS. On Monday morning The Psychotic approached me, and requested to know how the project was going. I was in the middle of explaining what I had done in the BSS, when The Psychotic suddenly and aggressively demanded to know "why I had not revisited the BRS". I found the anger and hatred in The Psychotic's manner to be utterly inexplicable. I explained carefully that I had only commenced the project at the end of last week, that as the BSS was urgently required I had given that priority, and accordingly I had worked all weekend on this document. The Psychotic's manner changed almost instantly to a strange attempt at humour.

This was the first example of what I later discovered to be the central principles of working in Vodafone Business Systems department.

1) The Psychotic develops an irrational hatred of anybody who works in the department.

2) With both a fear of, and unwillingness to communicate at even a basic level with members of the department staff, he fails continuously (and otherwise totally forgets) to inform staff of crucial information. He also perceives knowledge as some form of power over staff, and I have been informed that he at one time stated "I operate this department on a need to know basis" (an interesting rationalisation)

3) The fundamental repeated cycles of The Psychotic's character are :

i) The psychological need to demean every member of staff, and anybody else he perceives he has licence to.
ii) A complete lack of knowledge of what staff members have been doing, the level of effort that has been put into it, or any associated problems.
iii) At every opportunity to indulge in meaningless and ignorant confrontation. It is a depressing and regular occurrence that is the subject of much black humour within the department. It is characterised by one or two questions on a project, followed immediately by confrontational demands to put the recipient on the defensive. There then follows several minutes of accusations followed by defensive explanations, a very sick game that The Psychotic seems particularly to enjoy. This usually has to be followed with a further explanation until The Psychotic finally understands the issues.
iv) Confrontations are often followed by a weird sycophantic phase, which seem to have the purpose of reassuring The Psychotic that what he has just done has been forgiven.

4) The Psychotic has a total fear of anybody within the company who is at a senior (or sometimes equivalent) level. One of the unfortunate results of this is that the moment any problem arises, The Psychotic is gripped by this fear, and instantly has to find someone to blame. The usual order for this blame is i) a member of his own staff ii) another department. The Psychotic will always blame a member of his own staff first, and then if repeated explanations of the problem actually succeed,

The Psychotic will blame another department. Very often the problems are extremely minor, and very easily resolved.

5) The only real objective of the Business Systems department is the promotion of The Psychotic. I have been informed from several sources that The Psychotic has in the past stated openly to members of the Business Systems department that his salary increase is the only thing that matters. On one memorable occasion, apparently after receiving an increase, The Psychotic is reported to have stood in the middle of the office, triumphantly and repeatedly informing staff "I run this department for me."

Jo left the department in January 1996, shortly before I joined, having been frequently reduced to tears, having not spoken to The Psychotic for months, and having taken her case to Vodafone Personnel department.

Vanessa   I am quite sure did not really want to leave Vodafone (this view is shared by others). Shortly before she left I realised the level of her anger and frustration at what had occurred during her employment with Vodafone Business Systems. Only later did I realise the degree to which The Psychotic will play off one member of staff against another. There are two conversations between Vanessa and The Psychotic that I will remember for a long time.

The first four or five team meetings I attended were nothing but The Psychotic stating that "he had been receiving complaints about the department" and proceeding to blame and belittle everybody (except himself of course.)

Vanessa finally, desperately demanded to know why he did not stand up for members of the Business Systems department, a view totally backed by us all. The Psychotic replied "I do, I promote this department all the time."

What Vanessa really meant was "why do you sell us out all the time despite all the effort we put in to a very difficult job."
What The Psychotic meant was, " I promote me all the time. The more I can overload you with work, the more I can blame you, the better it will look for me."

The second memorable conversation was when Vanessa left. She had just started a major project (I think is was Pre-pay). At a small gathering at her desk, she looked at The Psychotic and in a final despair said something along the lines of "if you'd ever let me do just some of the things I wanted to do". The Psychotic's triumph at getting rid of Vanessa was obvious.

Mac had a total and utter contempt for The Psychotic. In return The Psychotic had a total hatred of Mac. At one team meeting apparently, The Psychotic had been attempting to explain something, and nobody present understood what on earth he was talking about. The Psychotic's anger was rising, and Mac pointed out that as six intelligent people had no idea what he was talking about, perhaps the fault lay with The Psychotic rather than with the staff. What followed has been described as The Psychotic attempting to give staff members 100 lines after school.

In retribution, The Psychotic appeared to do all he could to undermine Mac. I witnessed one episode where The Psychotic came out of his office, informed Mac that he had missed an important meeting that had started an hour before. Incredulously, Mac asked The Psychotic why he had not told him of the meeting an hour earlier. The Psychotic managed to be both confrontational and triumphant at the same time, but had no rational explanation.

I have no real knowledge of Mac's time at Vodafone, other than he was very helpful to me in his last couple of weeks. I am reasonably sure that Mac did not have a further contract at the time of his leaving. As he had young children and a family to support, I asked him whether he'd considered extending his contract at Vodafone, as there seemed to be far too much work as it was. I deduced that he would rather lose everything than work a moment longer than he had to in the vicinity of The Psychotic.

Throughout all this nightmare of the early months of my employment, two factors kept me determined to persevere with what was now looking a disastrous move to Vodafone. The first was one member of staff, who despite working unbelievable hours at office and home, had the patience to help both myself and another member of staff who had joined shortly after me. Without such help neither of us would have lasted a month. The second was the support and advice offered by a number of staff in other departments.

I then made what is possibly the worst business decision I have ever made.

Possibly one of the worst decisions I have ever made, was that if I was going to continue working at Vodafone, the only solution would be to attempt to communicate to The Psychotic the need to work together and to get the department up off its knees before it expired completely.

I have since had several illustrations that despite whatever efforts, support and backing any member of staff puts into this department, The

Psychotic is quite capable of selling them down the river at the first opportunity. Indeed, in desperation for approval from senior staff, that is quite often his first priority.

From my own experiences I have given only a few illustrative examples. I could quite easily cover pages more, but that would be pointless. More to the point, is that if my time to-date in Vodafone Business Systems has been so disgusting and obscene, it has been even worse for other members of staff, both past and present.

A few examples :

i) After successful completion of a Vodata project, I discovered I was required to make a presentation to Commercial Services. Late on the last day of the week, The Psychotic came over to my desk, without speaking, left a memo on my desk stating that I would be making the presentation the following Monday, and walked away again. Disbelieving, I looked at the memo, and wondered what on earth I was supposed to do. From many similar experiences since, I still cannot decipher whether this last-minute notice was because yet again The Psychotic had forgotten to pass on important information, or whether in fact it was deliberate. (I am aware that this last statement may seem unbelievable)

I spent the weekend getting what information I could off the Internet from the Vodafone Web Site, and putting a summary presentation together. I gave the presentation, which while not wonderful, seemed to be acceptable to the attendees at the meeting. One matter was raised, that of suspense records. One certain thing was that neither I, The Psychotic, or anybody else who had been involved with the project had considered this requirement until that point. The following morning I made the necessary enquiries, and completed a memo explaining the solution to the problem.

The Psychotic gave no feedback on the presentation. A day or so later, he approached me, and in a great rage made several unintelligible demands about suspense records and inter-network signalling costs (how anybody joining Vodafone and without any training or even communication is supposed to have instant experience of this I do not know). I informed him that after discussions with Vodata, the matter had been resolved, I was forwarding a memo to Vodata and Commercial Services, and that everybody was now seemed quite satisfied upon this point.

In the middle of the next week, The Psychotic approached me in sycophantic mode. He asked me what I had put in the memo, as he would like to put the same thing in a project he was concerned with.

ii) At the beginning of the Pre-Pay (then called Goliath) project, The Psychotic made totally unrealistic promises to senior management concerning schedules for documents. The business analyst who was working on it was already totally overloaded with work. I heard The Psychotic telling the analyst that he would have to work even longer hours, and he kept repeating in a panic "I would, I would". I was requested to work on some of the documents. On successive nights staff worked until the early hours of the morning. The Psychotic has never made even one comment of acknowledgement of the effort that was put in to fulfill his promises. After the other business analyst complained at the unreality of his workload, he was given several more projects.

iii) For months on end I worked endless evenings and weekends on my p.c. at home, meeting PAG deadlines. On each weekend I promised my family that I would not work the following weekend, and each successive weekend I broke the promise from the previous week. One weekend I said "I'm sick of this, this must be the seventh weekend in a row I've worked. My wife replied, "No it isn't, it's the ninth." I had by now come to realise like everybody else in the department that expecting any acknowledgement from The Psychotic was a waste of time, as his only concern was his annual pay rise.

In the middle of this I had my first performance review, which lasted 3.5 seconds. I had returned from a meeting, and was told to see The Psychotic in his office. I walked in. With a total hatred that shocked me after even all previous experiences, The Psychotic shoved a white envelope into my hand, and in a weird strangulated anger said "This is for you". End of meeting, end of review.

I walked back to my desk with the envelope, and somewhat stunned said to other members of the staff "Well, it looks like I've just been f****** fired !" I opened the envelope, and the first line of the enclosed letter said "Thank you for your efforts".

Some time later, I had arranged a meeting with The Psychotic, and during discussions he angrily told me that his pay rise had been reduced by 0.5% (for missing something I believe), and he was the only one who had lost money. I suddenly realised why the performance review months before had lasted 3.5 seconds.

I took over the project "Corporate Tariffs" which had been in progress for six months, with a BSS already issued for some time. No BRS had been issued throughout the project. The Psychotic had therefore been aware of this for six months, and had originally sanctioned a BSS without a BRS because of the urgency of the project.

The question of the BRS arose at the time of PAG approval (although in fairness the project was in something of a mess anyway). One afternoon The Psychotic approached my desk, and in a weird jokey way handed me a memo and said I've got to protect my back". The memo started "Once again Business Systems has been forced to rush out a BRS..."

That memo was either ridiculous or offensive, depending on your point of view. I lost track of the number of people from other departments who asked me "What's he trying to prove, who is he trying to blame this time, he's been in charge of this for six months .."

On the same project some time later, there occurred what I truly believe was an example of a fit of complete madness. The Psychotic had obviously received a phone call, concerning Mr. Tingey's attendance at a meeting on the project. The Psychotic came into the main office in a trance, stating "This could be escalated, this could be escalated ..". Neither I or anybody else had a clue what he was talking about. The Psychotic asked me about the meeting, and I informed him of the details.

From what he was trying to say, I asked him whether Mr. Tingey would be attending.

There followed two minutes of complete madness. In a fit, The Psychotic was yelling "I never said John Tingey wasn't coming, I never said that!" Other members of staff advised me to keep clear, as it was simply impossible to communicate with him in this state. In the middle of this a member of staff from Corporate Marketing came into the room, and witnessed the performance (ironically, The Psychotic had just stopped repeatedly shouting "What have Marketing got to do with it ?"). Afterwards this person asked me, laughing, "what was the matter, did he just get a phone call from John Tingey?" This episode went round more than one department, and yet again made Business Systems the object of derision and ridicule.

Immediately after this outburst, I phoned John Tingey's secretary who could not understand what all the fuss was about, and the meeting was confirmed within thirty seconds.

The next time the person from Corporate Marketing was in the office, The Psychotic approached with a nervous attempt at humour, to complete the inevitable cycle.

During two meetings on Corporate Tariffs, I attempted to discuss the requirement to understand something of Service Provider systems with regard to the project. Twice, this was dismissed, the second time with the remark that "these sort of things tend to waste time". The Psychotic later stated that he had never been to a Service Provider, in a manner that suggested that it would therefore be inappropriate for staff members of a lower rank to do so. At a later meeting which I had arranged with other departments, the requirement to investigate Service Provider systems was discussed, and a member of another department said "we need to get a couple of business analysts along", and named two people from their own department.

There have been endless problems ever since I started with lack of coordination between Business Systems and Marketing. The project "Gold & Chosen Numbers " is an extreme example of this. The Marketing Manager concerned made it quite clear that he was only using Business Systems because he had been told to do so, and anyway he had already done all the work for the implementation. It was also brought to the department's notice that the same Marketing Manager had been making derogatory comments about individuals in the department, and the department in general. This information was made known to The Psychotic, who said he would deal with it with Marketing.

The Psychotic went to Marketing, and informed them that in his view the Marketing Manager would make a very good business analyst. The Psychotic repeated this to me on his return. What more he could possibly have done to harm the Business Systems department is difficult to see. After further discussions, concerning meetings with other supportive departments, The Psychotic has now stated that he had not said this.

A recent team meeting (07/02/97) was beyond anything I could possibly describe. It contained everything. Confrontation followed by carefully repeated explanations on Corporate Tariffs, endless differing versions of what should and should not go in a BRS / BSS (some of them later hastily retracted by The Psychotic), attempts to blame members of staff for "failures" last year. When I informed The Psychotic that members of staff had worked until 2am, that at one time I worked nine weekends in a row, The Psychotic said that "he had not known what to do." If ever one meeting evidenced that Vodafone Business Systems is a rudderless ship, that was it. The Psychotic finally concluded with 'Tm just going to do what my boss tells me to. We are going to do BRSs and BSSs"

Following this meeting, I commenced the BRS for Mobile VPN Phase 2. The content and structure of this document were fully discussed before commencement. At a meeting on 14/02/97 a totally new document was produced by The Psychotic, which nobody else had previously seen, and to which the work was now supposed to have conformed. The work of the previous week had therefore been a complete waste of time.

There followed a discussion on this, and on the Business Systems department in general, which defied belief.

The last year has been one of complete and continuous conflict, with ever changing requirements and methodologies. No attempt has ever been made to resolve real problems. The Psychotic's definition of the purpose of the department, what the methodology is, what goes into documents - all this changes constantly depending on the latest problem. From recent questions to The Psychotic, it is quite clear that he does not even know what the role of business analysts in the department either is or should be.

One year ago, Vanessa was complaining bitterly about the lack of co-ordination with Marketing, the circumstances under which she had to work, the weird, disgusting and obscene behaviour of The Psychotic, and asking desperately "Why don't you stand up for this department."

One year later, it has simply got worse. It is my belief that when The Psychotic stated to members of staff "I run this department for me" he was for once consistent and accurate. Vodafone, Commercial Services, staff members or any other interest come a long way behind.

If the staff who have recently applied for jobs outside the department were successful, the complete department would have left in 11 months. A staggering fact is that it would not be the first time this has occurred.

Postscript.

At a recent meeting to discuss the new structure, and Business Systems role in that structure, an excellent summary of skills and requirements was put up on a whiteboard. It was pointed out that this was essentially what Vodafone's advertisements for Business Analysts had required, and that the work actually bore no relation to this (a fundamental reason for many problems). The Psychotic finally said that "he knew about this, but was concentrating on deliverables". Even The Psychotic's "new methodology" with which he is so obsessed, is actually an exact copy of what one staff member had been proposing six months ago. The Psychotic has no idea, and never has had, of the real work and the essential value of a business system department.

As usual, The Psychotic made many strange statements, blamed staff members, and at one juncture informed a staff member the "he did not know the way the business was going" followed by surreal comments about the MoU.

I have not documented the many conversations and phone calls I have had in my first year with members of other departments, including at a very senior level, about the department, which all reflect that the views of the company in general are the same as those within this department.

From being requested not to invite The Psychotic to meetings, to being informed that someone "nearly killed him" when yet again he claimed he had been trying to do something "for three years". I have lost track of the number of times that someone has successfully implemented something, and suddenly The Psychotic has been "trying to do this for three years."

An essential requirement for a Business Systems department is that it should not only work together within itself, but that it must work effectively with every other department. From the offensive obscenity of The Psychotic's mental instability, to the endless disgusting blame of every hard-working and professional person who has joined and then either left or attempted to leave, to the contempt and ridicule of other departments, Business Systems has never had the slightest chance of fulfilling its potential or proving it"s value to Vodafone. It is a department where mental instability, filth, cover-ups, blame, and lies are substituted for any form of competence.

Perhaps this year when The Psychotic wants to perform his weird dance to announce that Business Systems is run only for his benefit, perhaps he will perform it in an empty office from which all decent people have long since left.

End of Report

A short while after I got back The Psychotic marched over to me. He was triumphant, and handed me a memo. It was addressed to me, and copied only to one other person. Mr. Paul Wybrow. Yes, the very same Mr. Paul Wybrow.

Chapter 18 Genius

This is what The Psychotic wrote two hours *after* I had handed in my report. It is a work of genius. I admire people who are good at what they do, and the Psychotic was simply brilliant at being a Psychotic. What still astonishes me is that this fantastic deception was written when the Psychotic was near a total breakdown. If you care to ask a Clinical Psychologist, they may explain that such people can be immensely clever, and can plan the most complex deceits with the forward vision of a grand chess master. Because they have had a lifetime to perfect such skills.

INTERNAL MEMORANDUM

To: Jerry Nason
From: The Psychotic
cfi   Paul Wybrow
10 March 1997

I was concerned that at a meeting last week you made allegations that I do not support the department. This is not the first time and it is the second time within a short period when I have been counselling views on possibilities for a new methodology, that his has occurred.

It was unclear at the meeting whether this is a personal view or a team view. However, you were the only person at the meeting who voiced this opinion. However, it is obvious that you feel strongly about it and so the matter needs to be resolved.

No specifics were mentioned in the meeting, just generalities, although you did say that at one PAG I deliberately took on more work than the department could cope with (which PAG, what work?).

My experience is that the best way to resolve these problems is to get down to the specifics which support the view by documenting them; including the way in which I did not give this support. I ask that you list all occurances. In addition, I ask that you collate these on behalf of the department, if appropriate.

You intimated also that there are issues outstanding with other people and in particular, named John Tingey and Niall Garret. Would you please list all issues that you have with other people that are causing you problems with your work.

As I have done so in the past, I will take these matters up on your behalf and report the outcome back to you.

Finally, if you feel that I have been criticising you or the department unfairly for any reason, I would like you to document those specific instances also and to explain why you think the criticism was unfair.

It is apparent that these issues have been building up over a period of time. In future, could you either make these issues clear at the time, perhaps by putting them into writing, rather than let them accumulate.

Your reply will be treated in confidence.

Genius

Immediately following this, he took this memo of brilliant deceit to John Tingey and Niall Garrett, visited Nicki Hodgson, and phoned just about anybody I had ever had dealings with, and even some I had not.

What he was actually writing about was his own fears, but that was not the point. The point was of course that he'd been to see his friend Mr. Wybrow. I do not know whether they composed the memo together, but it is a distinct possibility. Because on the first page of my report, I detailed that one week before I `joined`, a fine woman had left in tears. The very woman that the Mr. Wybrow and the Psychotic had jointly got rid of. And the Psychotic and Mr. Wybrow had a few weeks before my report got rid of another fine young woman, with Mr. Wybrow grinning and shaking his head and saying "Don`t worry, we`ll get you back "

At two o`clock that afternoon, Mrs. Alison Stanton phoned me and said "Jerry, this is Alison. I know I gave you my word that nobody else would be involved, but Paul Wybrow said he`s going to investigate it". She sounded quite excited.

I am an old man, and an old fool, but not quite that stupid. Not so green as cabbage-looking, as one of my ancestors would have said.

From the moment of that call, I knew of course that everything was in vain. I had something of a desperation and anger and sadness, but I knew then that that was the end. I turned to Robert and said "she said `Paul Wybrow`s going to investigate it. I knew of course that in that empire of fear, if you said `this man is seriously disturbed`, you could not possibly stay there. The visit to Mrs. Alison Stanton had been one final, desperate gamble. One thousand to one shots rarely win. But I`m not that stupid. I had of course taken appropriate action in the event of disaster.

The ridiculous `investigation` duly took place. Mr. Wybrow was very, very nervous.

Mr. Wybrow "Erm, can I , erm ask you, how many people have seen this report ?"

Me. "Nobody. I asked a couple of people for their advice, but they`re not involved"

Mr. Wybrow "Erm, erm, are you in touch with previous members of the department ? "

Me. "Yes for example with Mac. (the man who had left in desperation a few weeks after I`d started).

I then gave descriptions of how this fine man had resorted to writing down everything The Psychotic had said, and then when a few minutes later asked The Psychotic "did you just say this?, The Psychotic would say `no, I never said that!".

By Mr. Paul Wybrow`s subsequent grinning, he was obviously very relieved. Nobody outside had seen the report, and I had not mentioned Jo, of whom he had got rid (what a terrible sentence). With his friend the Psychotic. And then got rid of another fine young woman. With his friend the Psychotic.

There was one truly astonishing part of the conversation. At one time I referred to `junior trainee cobol programmers.` It was a sarcastic reference to the fact that Vodafone`s advertisements for the `Business Systems` department were acts of Corporate Deceit.

One woman said "look at me, look at me. Look at what I`m doing." One man said "I thought I was coming here to ...". One man kept his initial job advertisement for two years, as a memento. Because of course the Psychotic had no idea what a business analyst department was there for, or what a `business analyst` was. But Vodafone`s `Personnel` department kept putting in advertisements of Corporate Deceit that had everything to do with a Psychotics fantasy, and nothing to do with reality.

And Mr. Paul Wybrow had even less idea than the Psychotic.

It took repeated explanations over thirty seconds at least to explain slowly and carefully to Mr. Paul Wybrow that the reference was a sarcasm. He really thought that people who had applied for positions in Business Analysis were instead working as junior trainee cobol programmers (no offence to programmers, I used to be one once.) And you will see in later chapters of this report that Mr. Wybrow copied the words of the Psychotic, and the real reason why together they decided it would be a good idea to change the name of the department.

During this `investigation` I received phone calls from a number of very fine people. "I`ve just had The Psychotic on the phone, he was ranting and raving. I told him the work you were doing to get departments to work together was good, but he just kept on ranting`.

Robert said. "You should have seen the look on their faces when I told them everything in your report was true." Fenella said "I told them everything was true but they just looked at me."

That afternoon, I was walking along a pavement in the small market town. On the opposite pavement was Niall Garrett. He seemed to be finding something very funny. I looked at him in some puzzlement. Just for good measure, I also encountered Paul Kerridge, who had the same demeanour. As I'd gone to considerable lengths to keep all of the report concerning The Psychotic confidential, it was not until much later of course that the penny dropped. Far too late. No pressing Button B to get my money back.

At four o'clock in the afternoon of the following day, I received a phone call from Alison Stanton "Erm, Jerry, would you, erm, be available at 5 o'clock this afternoon?" She sounded quite excited. I'm not that big a fool. As I left for the meeting, I turned to Robert who was such a fine man. "This is it", I said, "see you later. Thanks for your help."

"Come in Jerry"

Mrs. Alison Stanton and Mr. Paul Wybrow were in the office. They both seemed in a state of excited anticipation.
"Would you say you`ve lost all communication with The Psychotic ?" asked Mrs. Stanton.

I looked at them. Mrs. Alison Stanton looked quite excited, and Mr. Wybrow was grinning.

I looked at both of them. Such an obvious trap, I was suddenly very tired of all this amazing stupidity. "Would I say I`ve lost all communication ? Yes, of course."

They were jointly triumphant.

In Vodafone it is against the law to lose communication with a severely disturbed Psychotic who is further suffering from clinical depression, and who has the most debilitating fears shortly before he was to go to prison.. A dismissable offence.

Again, please pardon my inability to represent non-word sounds, but in the triumph of his deceit, Paul Wybrow conducted the remainder of the meeting grinning widely, and emitting a strange form of laugh that I have defined as "Ahoo"

"Ahoo, first time eh ?"

"Ahoo, bit of a shock eh ?"

"Ahoo, and we've been having complaints" I stared at this apparition, "Who ?" "Ahoo, Oh no, you kept everything confidential, so we're keeping everything confidential. Ahoo"

"This work you've been doing to get departments to work together, it's not the way forward."

"This work you've been doing to get the department to stand on it's feet. It's not the way forward."

"You're a caring person. Ahoo. You're a caring person" This was said as though it was some form of consolation prize. (part of this must have come from his discovery that my partner and I had visited the good young secretary in hospital. What a strange thing to do..) He knew absolutely nothing about me of course.

"Ahoo, I'll tell you what we're going to do. We've decided.... There followed details of a payoff. Just about enough to buy a small car,

Realising the reality of the triumph of his deceit, he continued "Ahoo, you can come back, you can come back, see the people in Business Systems. They like you, they like you."

And then he thought some more. "Ahoo, we'll say we mutually agreed to part, that's what we'll say" and sat grinning.

At this time I showed weakness and described how many `departments` had thanked me for my work. That was a moment of weakness which I regret, but now it's gone.. Paul Wybrow shook his head, grinning.

"What about all those people who went before " ?

"Ahoo, there's nothing I can do about that now."

"What about those people left behind "

Paul Wybrow sat silently grinning and shaking his head. I realised suddenly that the meeting was being recorded. It had to be, because if I'd got up and denied saying I'd "lost all communication" they had to have proof to ensure my departure that very afternoon.

I said "Does Vodafone care anything about people ? " Paul Wybrow continued to sit there, grinning and shaking his head. Mrs. Alison Stanton was quite excited. I'd have said sexually excited, but that's ridiculous.

I looked at both of them. You may imagine my countenance.

I said "There's another reason I have done this.". There was a continued silence, and continued grinning. How do you tell a man of such deceit and an excited woman who had given her word three times, how do you tell them that for some period of time a very accomplished Clinical Psychologist had made clear to me the nature of Psychosis. I will return to this fine man later, because he also brought great happiness to two people, almost inadvertently. I last heard him on Radio 4, so he must have achieved a wider recognition.

I thought about it, but only for a few seconds.

Again, as you may see from correspondence with Mrs. Alison Stanton, that meeting was recorded, because it had to be. It is why Mr. Paul Wybrow was very careful with his words, and mostly did grinning and silently shaking his head. It had been very well practiced or well rehearsed. You might almost think Mr. Wybrow had learned it by heart.

As I walked out I said incredulously to Mrs. Alison Stanton. *"Would you say you`ve lost all communication ?"*

"Oh I thought of that." Mrs. Alison Stanton was very excited and very proud. She was very excited and very proud that she had thought of that for Mr. Paul Wybrow and Vodafone Senior Management.

Then she added secretly, "he didn`t want to do it you know." In later parts of this report you will discover the very impressive extent of the deceit of Mr. Wybrow and the Psychotic. And how very recently I said to Mrs. Pauline Best "If Mr. Chris Gent had arranged that meeting, this could all have been concluded in half an hour.". And how I invited Mr. Gent to drinks by our pool to resolve this. But the Mr. Gent had no *direct* involvement in any of this.

May I ask you a favour?. Would you please re-read the transcript of that last meeting?. You may see that it has nothing to do with me and nothing to do with the Psychotic. You may see that Paul Wybrow simply and perfectly has defined himself. Can you imagine his fear when he first read my report? Can you imagine the release of his fear when I said "of course I've lost all communication". The "you can come back" for example was a naked projection of his own fears. The "we've been having complaints", was a direct copy of how the Psychotic opened every meeting. He had already been in the Empire of Fear for many years, and the labels and hierarchies and the empire were life itself. The grinning and shaking of the head were simply a denial of anything further that was said as though it was some strange game with utterly bizarre rules. I understand that before he joined Vodafone, Paul Wybrow had had a short unhappy time at a bank followed by a job running a chocolate machine.

The next morning, Paul Wybrow and the Psychotic stood in front of the Business Systems department and said they had tried so hard to find Jerry a position in another part of the company. Why, they had even gone back to Vodac.

Robert said to me " when the Psychotic spoke, he was suddenly saying "what do you think" to people, and people thought he had changed. But Robert was a very intelligent man, and said "but you could tell he hadn't really changed at all."

Paul Wybrow and Paul Sayers stuck their hands up the back of the Psychotic, as though he were some helpless dummy. And they made his mouth work and they told him the things to say. And the Psychotic in his fear obeyed.

And a few weeks later, Mr. Paul Wybrow stood stupidly in front of the `department` and said `does anybody know why he`s gone to prison?` Talking of careers, Mr. Paul Wybrow`s greatest good fortune was of course the very imprisonment of his friend The Psychotic. A wonderful career move.

Two days after my departure, I was speaking to Mrs. Alison Stanton on the phone.

"Actually Jerry, apart from the emotional bit, everything in your report was true, wasn`t it?". She was conspiratorial and almost giggly. The woman who had broken her repeated word to ensure that this was kept confidential with the deranged Psychotic, the woman who had potentially deprived my family of support, the woman who had betrayed every fine member of that department past and present, actually whispered to me, conspiratorially and giggly.

"Actually Jerry, apart from the emotional bit, everything in your report was true, wasn`t it?".

(I presume the `emotional` bit was the statement that if perhaps next year The Psychotic danced in the middle of the room repeatedly shouting "I run this department for me !   I run this department for me !", perhaps he may be dancing in an empty room from which all others have long since departed.)

She also wrote very cheerily "I hope your search for alternative employment is going well, and please do not hesitate to contact me if you feel I can be of any assistance to you." Wasn't that nice of her.

A few weeks later, after The Psychotic's imprisonment, I was driving back from the airport. I phoned Mrs. Alison Stanton, (yes, I know it`s illegal, and I`ve never done it since). "I`d like to make an appointment to see you Alison" I said. The mobile phone relayed the naked fear. Fear is a very strange element. You can see it, and you can literally smell it. And you can hear it in a voice of a woman of no self-worth over a mobile telephony network.

"No I can`t. No I can`t. I`ve got appointments and meetings for the next weeks. I can`t arrange anything else !"

I could almost feel sorry for Mrs. Alison Stanton, but not quite. Can you imagine how Paul Wybrow and the Psychotic and Paul Sayers must have laughed at her?. They had conspired to cover up the fact that Vodafone`s empire of fear and hierarchies and labels had employed a Psychotic for many years. They had deceived her, and used her, and put all the responsibility on to her.

Mrs. Alison Stanton had a label of self-worth. She was a *Senior* Personnel Officer. That was her label. Many people from Business Systems paid a high price for that label.

Chapter 19 Psychosis

The trouble with Psychotics is that they do not know that they are psychotic.

A Psychotic may go next door and burn the house down. When you say to the Psychotic, "why did you burn the house down ?", they will reply "I did not burn the house down." Within their beings, from then on they did not burn the house down. If you show them the rubble, they will shake their head and state that it has been nothing to do with them. To you and I this is the most preposterous lie. To the Psychotic it is simply the truth.

After my departure, on the phone, Jo said "you wanted to go in there (his office) and just shake him!" But you make shake a Psychotic for ever and it will make no difference, for a very good reason. At the end of this report I would like just to summarise what I learned from a Clinical Psychologist. It was nothing to do with Vodafone, and nothing to do with the reasons of our meetings. It just evolved over two years.

And Psychotics are the most glorious of catalysts.

In system design, a common approach is to define three layers. The presentation layer, the business logic, and the data layer.

I have come to think that this could most aptly be applied to human beings. The data layer is all of our inheritances and our learning as we grow. The data of our nature and nurture. The logic layer is how we learn to translate and use that data and deal and interact with the world for what we wish to do. The presentation layer is the front we present to the world. We are as a species, very clever at the presentation layer.

With their fear, cunning, and expertise in deceit you may often find that a Psychotic is a glorious catalyst who causes the falseness of our presentation layers to crumble so that we may see the real being beneath.

Chapter 20   Career Moves

Immediately after the imprisonment of the Head of Business Systems at Vodafone, everybody said "this makes Paul Wybrow look a complete fool."

Immediately after the imprisonment of the Head of Business Systems at Vodafone, the best description of Paul Wybrow was given by a fine man.

"Arrogant and disinterested."

Disinterested, because he had not a clue what the Business Systems department was supposed to do, with his chief partner now Mr. Marcus Cox.

Arrogant, because he'd already been advised that at a suitable time he would be promoted out of there. It is a very old tactic, dating back to military time of long ago. They could not get rid of him, because that would have declared previous Corporate guilt. They could not leave him there, for there were many people who knew the background. So the solution was simple.

After a suitable couple of months, Mr. Paul Wybrow, with the full agreement of all of the Directors of Vodafone, was 'promoted' out of the way, to become a "Director of Vodafone International." Corporate power in an Empire of Fear, and a lesson to others.

One man said to him that before he went to prison, the Psychotic had promised him a pay rise. Paul Wybrow sneered arrogantly at him "You don't want to believe everything that he said, do you?" Arrogance is the coat of choice for the grossly inadequate.

What a wonderful career move. As a severely ill human being collapsed into complete disintegration in a prison cell, the weight of his despair bearing down on one side of the see-saw ensured the other side rose to project the other human to a high position.

Later, when my website describing these events became known within Vodafone, by a strange coincidence. Paul Wybrow was moved to a position in Belgium

Later still, when one of my companies won a contract at that company in Belgium, by a strange coincidence Paul Wybrow was promoted back to high office in the U.K.

Career moves.

Chapter 21   We've moved on.

I next phoned Mrs. Alison Stanton, a few weeks later.

"Listen Alison, I want to keep this between you and me, o.k.? All I want is to ensure that the true facts are established. "

"Yes, Jerry, o.k. "

"Alison, we must keep this confidential."

"Yes, Jerry o.k. "

As soon as she put the phone down she went straight to the Senior Management, and more pertinently to another Manager who was now in charge of some of the good people involved.

Ask Mrs. Alison Stanton what she did next, discover the harm it caused to good people, and ask her about the day she suddenly took as holiday.

Finally, I managed to arrange a meeting with Alison Stanton, though not with other people involved as "they could not attend during working hours".

Following is an extract from my last recorded meeting with Mrs. Alison Stanton :

"Come in Jerry, take a seat. Can I ask you to summarise what you want to get out of this meeting?"

I summarised.

I will not bore you with the rest of the conversation, as the only purpose of the meeting, the only reason it had been allowed to proceed was to enable Vodafone to gain knowledge of how much I might know, be able to prove, and what I intended to do. A few sentences are worth repeating.

I asked "What would you suggest we should have done?" (The 'we' being the giggling lover Marcus Cox, Peter Chapman who just sat there exuding filth, the mousey secretary who just sat there in the reflected power, two good people, the new person and this despairing old man.)

Mrs. Stanton thought. Then she thought some more. Then she thought harder. Suddenly she had the answer. "You could have come as a group" she announced proudly.

Then, totally out of context :

"Well, the Psychotic, he's not coming back to Vodafone!" (It was common knowledge that If Paul Sayers had still been in charge, there was a real possibility that the Psychotic would have been re-employed, not least for the purposes of continuing the cover-up.)

"As for Paul Sayers, we've moved on." (The indoctrinated "we".)

"As for John Tingey, nnnnhig !"

Me : "Mr. Wybrow was involved in the departure of at least two people from that `department`"
Mrs. Alison Stanton is puzzled and replies "How could he have been, he was new to that department ?"

"Could you tell me Alison why none of the procedures in your handbook `Working Together` were followed ? "

Mrs. Alison Stanton stares blankly, as though this is the first time she has realised it.

She says : "Well, Mr. Wybrow said .... ", and then stops herself.

"He didn't last long did he ?"

I believe that at this point Mrs. Alison Stanton understood everything. At last. There are a million ways to say a sentence, a million ways to utter a Corporate Phrase. She was staring blankly, and said slowly "We didn't want to lose him." A woman of no self-worth uttering a Corporate Phrase she'd been taught, that she no longer believed in.

Silence, then "This could cause trouble for you at your new employment". This was said with considerable spite.

"Why could it cause trouble, Alison ? What I'm doing now has nothing to do with Vodafone`.

Silence.

"No, I suppose not."

"This could cause trouble for you at your new employment". A corporate phrase uttered many months later by an obedience-dog named John Tingey after he followed a very fine man into a bookshop in a small market town in England. They must have had meetings on how to threaten the welfare of my family.

On my last day at Vodafone, as I walked into the room, the wonderful trick question was "Would you say you've lost all communication with the Psychotic ?" And Mrs. Alison Stanton was so excited and so proud that she had thought of it.

Except of course that she did not think of it at all.

During the 'investigation' the Psychotics` secretary said "Oh, I told them he couldn`t communicate".

I`ve met the finest of women upon this earth. What they would think of Vodafone`s `Personnel` department I cannot imagine.

At that last recorded meeting I said to Mrs. Alison Stanton :

"Could you tell me Alison why so many people warned me against going to `Personnel` ?"

"I don`t know why", she said indignantly, "we`ve got grievance procedures!"

As I was driving back, I could not help laughing at this surreal and wonderful idiocy. And then I remembered. Then I remembered. There is part of this report that is inaccurate. My excuse is that as I have operated under a different label, I have never before or since had any dealings with `Personnel` departments. I`ve omitted to tell you something.

"Mrs. Stanton, this is very important. It concerns The Psychotic."

"Oh yes, what is it ?"

"I cannot hand this over unless you give me your word that nobody else will be involved. I don`t care what happens to me, but nobody else must be involved. It is very important".

"What is it ? *Is this a grievance procedure*"

*"What ? It doesn`t matter, this is so important.* "It`s a report on one year at Vodafone, but it`s about The Psychotic. It is very important that nobody else is involved. I am not going to hand this over unless you give me your word that this will be kept between us and The Psychotic.

I didn't fill out the correct form. Mr. Gent had no direct involvement.

I phoned one time later, and was told that Mrs. Alison Stanton was unavailable as she was conducting a Graduate Intake meeting. The woman who had broken her word so many times, who had brought harm to good people, the woman who had sat there excited as Paul Wybrow said "This work you've been doing to bring the departments together, it's not the way forward Ahoo !", the woman who had threatened "This could cause trouble for you at your new employment", this is the woman who welcomed our children into Vodafone.

And as she greeted our children with a smile, she handed them Vodafone's corporate handbook. It's title was "Vodafone - Working Together".

Chapter 22 Even more boring

Dear reader, if you thought that these pages up to now have been boring, wait until you have to read the remainder. All that follows now is a description of meetings, correspondence which duplicates what has gone before, and a description of how Vodafone were able to suppress all free speech and illegally close down discussion websites.

The only purpose for reading the remainder of this publication is if you have any interest in for example, the concepts of the Internet as a wonderful invention for responsible free speech for all of the world. Or if you wish to learn how to close down a website. Depends which side you are on.

It also details how the future 'Lifetime President' of Vodafone wrote a letter of 4 sentences with 2 deceptions in it. And how the author of this tome came finally to realise that in such empires of fear, it is not what you know, but the part you decide to play.

If you do care to read on, I would further like to propose to you a view of our world, and to ask whether you are in agreement. I would like to propose to you that if you examine the structure, morals and motivation of this empire, you may see that it is no different from any other such empire. The only difference may be the cloth uniforms. If you examine the extreme inter-departmental racism, you may see that it is no different from standard racism. If you observe the behaviour of the 'departments' it is no different from how we still divide our beautiful world into departments and races and religions. If you observe the caste system, you may see that it is no different from every other caste system that humans have employed for thousands of years. Concepts of time and place.

Otherwise, throw this book aside now, and may I wish you a pleasant day.

Chapter 23 In one letter.

Sometime after my departure I, and a couple of others, arranged a meeting of past "Business Analysts" who had been through the nightmare of Vodafone's "Business Systems" department. What came out was that the same cycles of madness had been going on for a long, long time. We discussed the environment, the filth, and there were of course common themes - John Tingey was for example universally regarded with disgust, and Nial Garrett was the subject of much derision. What amazed me was the purity of Niall Garrett's racism. Every person who joined Vodafone's Business Systems had the same story of his deliberate sabotage of their work, and his pleasure in doing so because of his hatred of the Psychotic.

The new man was not able to make the meeting, but sent me a letter. In one letter he has summarised everything of that place.

To: Jerry N   Technical Author

From: Jonathan L
Pedantic Git   12th August 1997

BUSINESS ANALYST MEETING

This meeting is unacceptable for attendance from a pedantic git point of view for the following reasons :-

1. It was not my idea, so it cannot be any good;

2. It may involve some effort on my part;

3. You did not ask me first, so I don't feel important enough;

4. I am paranoid that I might be seen doing something helpful;

5. You did not specify the map reference of the meeting location;

6. You did not specify what I should wear, including underpants, sock and shoelaces (if required);

7. You may discuss advanced high technology issues relating to your current role, about which I am ignorant and about which I may be jealous.

8. My esteemed colleague and a man to whom many Vodafone staff owe an enormous debt of gratitude, Marcus Cox, may be the subject of slander and ridicule which I would find distasteful.
Kind Regards
Jonathan

p.s. what do you mean by meeting ? Are you intending to convey the fact that a group of people (male and female), who share a common interest, will discuss topics that relate to that interest in an open and convivial manner, pausing occasionally for an alcoholic beverage or for a bite to eat ?

If so, why not say so ?

There was of course much discussion of the Psychotic, which does not need to be repeated here. One common theme was the total indoctrination, the reason that the Psychotic had found his home. Statements were always commenced with the indoctrinated 'we'. "We don't mind how many subscribers we add, as long as it's more than Orange. "We think that the share price will go to two pounds fifty". And very often he would emerge from the office shouting the share price rise, as though he were instrumental in it's increase.

The indoctrinated 'we'.

The same indoctrinated 'we' as for example with Alison Stanton. "As for Paul Sayers, we've moved on"

The same indoctrinated "we" as the devious and grinning Paul Wybrow "I'll tell you what we are going to do".

The same indoctrinated "we" as a young lady from Vodafone's legal department used "We think this matter is in the past now".

The same indoctrinated "we" as the woman who said "We go to lunch at 12.30 and return at 1.30"

It was their place, their home.

I spoke to Jo on the phone. When discussing Vodafone, there was still the same disgust in her voice as with every other person who had been through there. "They tried to get me to back there, but I wasn't going back there, I'm a Business Analyst." It was the same statement as all professional people who had discovered the truth of that place. With bitterness, "That Paul Wybrow, he's useless, he's useless.... and he's useless at.. "

In Vodafone, the empire of fear and hierarchies, the Psychotic was valued higher than all of the professional people who had been through there put together. Levels and caste systems. Nobody understood this better than the Psychotic.

Chapter 24 Mr. K

Most of the rest of this book is concerned with correspondence, and contains the name of the Psychotic in many places. I do not wish this man's name to be known publicly, for it is not my aim to bring further harm to him and any family he may have. He was not evil, he was very ill, and had very little control over his actions.

The likes of the devious Paul Wybrow had every control over what they did. Paul Wybrow and Chris Gent had been given so many opportunities to resolve this privately, and if they had done so this book would never have been published. But in their cowardice and their corporate arrogance, they have evaded all attempts at resolution, and have been well protected by the Corporation.

To continue substituting his name with "The Psychotic" would not be realistic, so I have simply changed all references to Mr. K

Following is an extract of a letter I wrote to Winchester Crown Court.

June 1997

Winchester Crown Court, Law Court, Winchester, Hampshire SO23 9ELDear Sirs,

Re. Mr. K

Further to my recent telephone call, I would be most grateful if you could provide me with information on the recent case concerning Mr. K. I understand that Mr. K was sentenced to two years in prison at Winchester Crown Court, in March or April of this year, and that the matter concerned an assault

Until his conviction, Mr. K was the manager of the Business Systems department at Vodafone. I joined that department in February 1996 as a Business Analyst. Within five weeks of my joining, two members of staff (out of four) had left the department, and I discovered a further young lady had left in tears the week before I joined. I was also advised that a number of people had left in the year preceding my joining.

On several occasions I attempted in private to discuss with Mr. K his irrational hatred of anybody who ever joined the department, and the harm that was caused to both them and the department. It was my view that Mr. K was a very disturbed person who sort refuge in lies and blaming members of staff, and this view was shared by the other staff. In January of this year I wrote a report on my first year in Vodafone, and asked two other members of staff to verify the content.

Very reluctantly, I handed this to Mr. K in February of this year, in an attempt to get him to discuss matters with a representative of the Personnel department. Mr. K immediately wrote a completely false memo, and without the knowledge of anybody in the department, commenced a campaign of lies and deceit. This resulted in my being fired a few days later.

Neither I, or anybody else of course, had any knowledge that Mr. K" s impending court case. In hindsight, part of Mr. K's desperate measures were no doubt in fear of disclosure of the facts concerning his behaviour, shortly before the hearing.

I also wrote that I would like to visit Mr. K in prison.

The Court responded that they were unable to provide information, but I did receive a letter from Mr. K from the prison. It read :

"Dear Jerry,

The Prison Authorities have advised me that you have requested to visit me. Unfortunately, visits are few and far between, and I use them for family and close friends.

I am unaware as to why you would like to visit, but it is possible for you to write to me at the above address."

With kind Regards

Mr. K

Chapter 25   Fine men to have on your side.

I wrote to Mr. Chris Gent, future Lifetime President :

STRICTLY PRIVATE AND CONFIDENTIAL
Mr. Chris Gent,
Vodafone Ltd.,
The Courtyard,
2-4 London Road,
Newbury,
Berkshire RG14 1JX

Dear Mr.Gent,

Please find enclosed a copy of my last letter to Mrs. Alison Stanton.

I have made an appointment with Mr. Paul Wybrow, which I am sure he will wish to attend. It is most important that the events concerning Mr. Paul K, and the principles that they illustrate, are accurately recorded.

Yours sincerely,

Guess whether Mr. Wybrow turned up at this most important meeting?

Dear Mr. Wybrow,

Several weeks ago we made an appointment to record your answers to critical questions concerning your actions with regard to your friend, the clinically psychotic Mr. K, shortly before he was sentenced to two years imprisonment

Three days before the arranged appointment, I phoned to confirm this most important meeting, as was informed, hesitantly, that you would be unavailable, as you 'had a conference call booked'. I had booked my flight to the U.K. especially for this meeting, and I would never otherwise have learned of your convenient and coincidental 'conference call' until my arrival.

Nevertheless, we may now resolve some key issues, by comparing your written responses to the information recorded from a number of sources,

I am sure that you will understand the great importance of your replies, as they will be accurately recorded in the document to be distributed to the staff, directors, and shareholders of Vodafone, both in the U.K. and abroad.

A short time before my arrival at Vodafone, you were involved, together with your friend Mr. K, in the departure, in tears, of a valued member of the Vodafone 'Business Systems' department. Please describe briefly your part in those events.

We wrote a summary of one year at Vodafone, and went to seek Vodafone Personnel's help with regard to your friend Mr. K's severely psychotic behaviour.

Two hours later he wrote a completely fabricated memo, copied only to you. Can you suggest any reason why he might have done this ?

Despite Mrs. Alison Stanton's repeated assurances to me that our summary should be discussed with Mr. K only, you persuaded Mrs. Stanton that you were going to 'investigate it'. Could you explain briefly why you did this? Can you please explain why this was never discussed with Mr. K, the whole point of our efforts on behalf of staff members of that department ?

The document of course on its first page, mentioned the departure of the valued member of staff, in who's departure you had been involved with your friend Mr. K.

During our meeting you very concerned with which previous members of that department we had contact. Would you please explain the reason for your concern.

After Mr. K had written to you a completely fabricated memo, he commenced a desperate campaign of lies and deceit. It was later discovered that he had additional motives for this, as had our statement become public, he might have been sentenced (deleted). Would you clearly state what knowledge you had of your friend Mr. K's activities between the time he copied to you his memo, and our last meeting.

Would you please explain why my statement, and Mr. K's fabricated memo written two hours later, were never further discussed.

A short time before my arrival at Vodafone, you were involved, together with your friend Mr. K, in the departure, in tears, of a valued member of the Vodafone 'Business Systems' department. Would you explain why, in your supposed 'investigation', you failed to inform Mrs. Alison Stanton, or anybody else, of your involvement.

In your 'investigation', you failed to inform members of other departments of the basis of, and the events leading up to, this 'investigation'. Would you please explain this most serious omission.

You had it confirmed to you by the two other longest-serving members of that department, that the contents of our statement were completely accurate. You also had descriptions of Mr. K's psychotic fits that were on the edge of extreme violence, examples of his very complete incompetence, examples of his inability to understand even the simplest of concepts, examples of his gross inadequacy as a human being, and examples of the fact that he was a compulsive liar. Would you please explain to the staff, directors, and shareholders of Vodafone why, after your bizarre question 'Would you say you've lost communication with Paul K', that you then found the remainder of the meeting very amusing.

The full (this time the very full) transcript of that final meeting is recorded accurately in the report to be distributed. Incidentally, Mrs. Stanton was told at our last recorded meeting "Paul Wybrow was involved in the departure of at least two people from that department." She is puzzled, and replies "but he was new to that department" followed by silence. She is then asked "Why do you think Mr. Wybrow was grinning and shaking his head?".

You were informed that there was another reason I had made the statement. It is concerned with the fact that I sought professional advice concerning the nature of psychopathic behaviour. A few weeks before my departure, while I was talking to some other staff members, your friend Mr. K, whom you had so ably and deviously protected, said "Women are no trouble if you hit them", and laughed.

At our last meeting, my last three questions were ;

"What about all those people who went before ?" You replied, grinning and shaking you head, "There's nothing I can do about that now"

"What about those people left behind ?" You were silent, grinning and shaking your head.

"Does Vodafone care anything about people ?" You were again silent, continuing to grin and shake your head.

Would you please inform the staff, directors, and shareholders of Vodafone why your friend Mr. K was sentenced to two years imprisonment, four weeks later.

Yours sincerely.

Copy to Mr. C. Gent

No reply was, of course, ever received from this fine man.

Chapter 26 Gent the Gent

I further tried writing to Mr. Gent, the future Lifetime President of Vodafone. I thought he would be a true gent, and respond in a positive fashion.

STRICTLY PRIVATE AND CONFIDENTIAL
Mr. Chris Gent,
Vodafone Ltd.,
The Courtyard,
2-4 London Road,
Newbury,
Berkshire RG14 1JX

Dear Mr.Gent,

Please find enclosed a summary of events surrounding my departure, and the departure of Mr. Paul K shortly thereafter upon his conviction and imprisonment. I also enclose a copy of a recent letter to Mrs. Allison Stanton.

As Mrs. Stanton is aware, I have been trying for the last year to simply ensure that the events of that time, and the very serious issues raised, are accurately recorded.

I would very much welcome a brief meeting with yourself, and any other interested parties, in order to ensure that all of the relevant facts concerning Mr. Paul K, and the history of the `Business Systems` department may be confirmed.

I would confirm that I have no interest other than the establishment of the truth, in order that the matter may be finally resolved and consigned to history.

Yours sincerely,

J.N

No response was received. Of course.

So I tried again :

Mr. Chris Gent,
Vodafone Ltd.,
The Courtyard,
2-4 London Road,
Newbury,
Berkshire RG14 1JX

Dear Mr.Gent,

Further to correspondence of some time ago, I would be most grateful if you could provide me with the following information concerning the imprisonment of Mr.K, and the promotion of Mr. Paul Wybrow. This information can then be published, and Mrs. Best may proceed to further investigate this matter internally.

Would you please advise whether you were informed of the imprisonment of Mr. K the then 'Head' of Vodafone Business Systems Department, and if so, on what date this advice was first given.

Would you please advise the date of Mr. K's departure from Vodafone.

Would you please advise the date it was decided to 'promote' Mr. Paul Wybrow.

Would you please advise whether Mr. Paul Wybrow's 'promotion' was sanctioned, promoted, or otherwise agreed to by yourself.

Yours sincerely,

J.N.

No response was ever received. Of course.

So the same question was asked of Mrs. Pauline Best, the future "Global People Development Director". The response was :

Dear Mr N

I acknowledge receipt of your letter dated 6th February 1999 received 11th February 1999. You have not given any details as to why you require the information regarding Mr Paul Wybrow and his promotion to Director.

114

As you probably know, information of the type you seek is in the public domain and is available from Companies House.

I am anxious to bring this matter and sequence of correspondence to a conclusion and if you have any views on how this may be achieved, please let me know.

Yours sincerely

Pauline Best

It would have been simpler and quicker for Mrs. Best to have named the date. But of course she just avoided the issue. If you are Global People Development Director in an empire of fear, you can do that.

Mrs. Pauline Best had written, "Paul Wybrow and John Tingey will not answer your questions", and also banned all communications from myself with Vodafone personnel. But I thought I would carry on trying, and have faith in fine people. So I wrote again to Mr. Gent :

Private and Confidential

Mr. Gent,

As usual, copies herewith for information (this is getting wearying, isn't it?) . Sometime, somewhere in Vodafone there has to be someone with the intelligence and independence to understand the fundamental issues. Let's hope it's Pauline Best.

I think the ban on communications refers only to employees. If you'd like to come to dinner one evening or for drinks by the pool, that would be fine by us if its o.k. with you.

Regards,
JN

No reply was ever received. Of course.

Chapter 27 The Meeting

There is much correspondence leading up to my meeting with Mrs. Pauline Best which I will not bore you with. After much to-ing and fro-ing, and "this won't happen unless", and all sorts of other trivia, I finally got to a meeting with Mrs. Pauline Best and a Mrs. Frazer-King of Vodafone's legal department.

I had been asked to provide an agenda, so this is what I came up with, with a request for some further information.

1. Proposed Agenda

It is proposed that each section is strictly limited to the specified time, and that any outstanding issues within each section then remain unresolved. The objective of each section is to obtain mutual agreement.

Item	Time
Summary of the events immediately leading up to my initial visit to Mrs. Alison Stanton, and immediately thereafter.	5 minutes
The last meeting with Mrs. Alison Stanton and Mr. Paul Wybrow.	5 minutes
Confirmation by yourself that you fully endorse the content and procedure of that meeting.	1 minute.
The subsequent actions of Mrs. Alison Stanton	5 minutes
The involvement of Mr. Paul Wybrow in the 'Business Systems' department, from before my joining Vodafone, to the time of his 'promotion'.	5 minutes
Summary of the actions taken by myself over the course of two years in this matter.	2 minutes
Summary of actions by yourself in this matter.	2 minutes
Confirmation by yourself that you fully support the actions and behaviour of Mrs. Alison Stanton, and your Personnel department and procedures.	1 minute.

Confirmation by yourself that the staff of Vodafone may have your complete assurance that, as Human Resources Director, you fully endorse and support Mr. Paul Wybrow.	1 minute.
Summary, and mutual agreement on the actions which must now be taken.	3 minutes.

The complete meeting will therefore take no more than thirty minutes, and in view of the effort I have put in over such a long time to ensure that matters are accurately recorded, I am sure we will both wish to make this meeting as open and constructive as possible. The resultant will be no further need for any correspondence, and the understanding that any and all subsequent actions will be mutually understood to be inevitable.

Requests for further information.

I would be most grateful if you would provide the following important information at or before the meeting :

Would you please obtain a brief summary by Jane Boiston of why she phoned Mr. Paul K immediately after the visit by Jo (shortly before I joined Vodafone.)

In order to escape from the nightmare of the 'business systems' department, I applied for a position with Vodac. I am not for one minute suggesting that I was in any way the best candidate for the position, and that is of course irrelevant. However the following is crucially important, and is at the centre of important events both before and after. Would you please obtain confirmation from both other parties involved in that interview, that Mr. Paul K, either directly or indirectly through his past association with other members of staff, effected no input into that process.

Would you please provide the name and position of the person who re-employed Mr. Paul Sayers on contract.

After Mr. Paul K's imprisonment, and Mr. Paul Wybrow's 'promotion', as part of the cover-up, Jo was later encouraged to accept a position back with Vodafone. Would you please confirm the source of that invitation.

Would you please provide the date that Mrs. Alison Stanton was 'promoted' to 'Senior Personnel Officer'.

Many thanks.

Mrs. Pauline Best, Global People Development Director, wrote to say that she had decided that all of the answers to the above questions "were confidential" and she hoped I would understand that.

I entered the meeting room with Mrs. Best and Mrs. Frazer-King.

"You have to understand this was before my time", said Mrs. Best. The get-out clause.

"Could we ask you what is the real purpose of your continuing actions ?"

"Two reasons. One is to ensure that the events of that time are accurately recorded. And secondly, no person, particularly no young person, should ever walk into something like that. That's why I went to such lengths to get Mr. K to examine what he did with an independent person in private"

Mrs. Best looked at me. "And who was that person" she asked with interest.

I sat there gawping. "What ?"

"And who was that person" she repeated.

"Why, Mrs. Alison Stanton of course" I replied in disbelief. "I went to see her, I said I didn't mind what happened to me, but it was absolutely essential that this was kept just between us."

Mrs. Pauline Best did not know it was Mrs. Alison Stanton I had gone to see. Some time earlier Mrs. Pauline Best had written :

"I am responding to your letter addressed to Mr Gent and he has asked me to deal with this in my capacity as Personnel Director for Vodafone Limited.

Your request, in summary, is to ensure that the circumstances surrounding your departure are accurately recorded. I can confirm that.

In conclusion, we have noted the contents of your letter. We feel that no further action is necessary and would like to close this matter.

Hopefully, you will agree with this action and feel that this matter has been dealt with satisfactorily."

We will never know what she was told at that time, or what further deceits were practiced.

The meeting progressed and none of my agenda items were properly addressed.

At one stage I informed her "Mrs. Best, you have the responsibility for the welfare of all those people out there. "I know what my responsibilities are!" she thundered. The presentation layer slipped for a moment.

At one stage they left the room for five minutes. On one side there was a brochure extolling the merits of young people joining Vodafone's `IT` or `Project Management` departments. I will never know whether it was left there deliberately. It said "Vodafone is a mature company in a new industry", or words to that effect. Vodafone is not of course a `mature` company. It is a very, very old company. It dates back to at least the youth of Gerald Whent, and much further.

The brochure on the side said `there are structures but they are there to help your career.` Or something similar.

I informed them that I intended to publish my report. Mrs. Best did not look too happy. "May I ask where you are going to publish it" she asked. "I think that's confidential" I said. The irony was lost on her. In any case, I had already used my website address at that time. It was called fmicom, as I had a passion for mobile and fixed integration at that time, so they knew full well where I would publish it.

Mrs. Best assured me that she would fully investigate further and let me know, so I agreed to wait.

Sometime later, I wrote to Mrs. Best to say that to ensure the integrity of the investigation, would Mr. Chris Gent simply answer the questions concerning Mr. Paul Wybrow's promotion, and would Mr. Wybrow please answer the questions in my previous communication. Once open and honest responses had been received, Mrs. Best could complete her investigations in private, and no further harm to anybody could result. The only alternative I had was to publish my report.

Shortly after I received a communication from Mr. Chris Gent, future Lifetime President.

Vodafone Airtouch
Chris Gent
Chief Executive
24 August 1999

I write in response to your letter dated 15 August 1999.

I have forwarded this correspondence to Mrs. Pauline Best whom I believe you met on Monday, 19 April 1999, together with Mrs. Fraser-King of Vodafone's Legal Department.

I have asked Mrs. Best to deal with this matter on my behalf. I had no direct involvement with any of the matters to which you refer and I am confident that Mrs. Best is doing her utmost to address your concerns and deal with this matter in a way which is satisfactory to both yourself and Vodafone.

I would be most grateful if you would direct all future correspondence to Mrs. Best.

Yours sincerely

As you may see, the statements "I had no *direct* involvement" and ""I am confident Mrs. Best is doing her utmost to address your concerns" are unfortunately both economical with the truth. A number of people have interpreted the statement "in a way which is satisfactory to both yourself and Vodafone" as an invitation to keep it quiet in return for some reward, but that is mere conjecture.

At the same time Mrs. Best wrote in a similar manner.

Later after Vodafone illegally closed down the discussion forum, I wrote to Mr. Gent :

A short while later, I received on the same day, a letter from yourself, and a letter from Mrs. Best. If you were aware already of the existence of the forum, then Mrs. Best`s letter is one of considerable deceit, and your letter to me was prompted by the fear of publication. You have on several occasions refused to arrange a meeting to discuss the events, including an invitation from my family, and diverted all enquiries. Why you should then have been motivated to write that letter is best left to independent observers.

No reply was ever received. Of course.

There was much correspondence with Mrs. Alison Stanton, all of which was met with evasion. A few weeks after the meeting I phoned Mrs. Alison Stanton and decided to be authoratative. Impressive or what. In a very authoratative manner I demanded "You have failed to answer any of the questions."

"I, I've been away having a baby" she faltered. And then she said, sort of accusingly, "While I was away you went to see Mrs. Best. " It was as though she was blaming me for harm that had come to her. I realised that she must have been dragged into Mrs. Best's office and interrogated concerning Mrs. Best sitting there like a stunned mullet when I informed her that it was Mrs. Stanton I had gone to see. Tangled webs.

Suddenly she remembered what she'd been told to say. "You, you must go through our legal department" she said.

I could almost feel sorry for Mrs. Stanton. But not quite. The parents of the Psychotic were apparently in touch with her. I must apologise to these parents for this inclusion. Can you imagine the pain that must be inside you if one of your children was sent to prison. Can you imagine the despair, the tears, the sleepless nights, the numbing emptiness. In their pain, they had apparently said to her "nobody thought he would go to prison." This is an understandable attempt at rationalising what is beyond pain. Mrs. Stanton announced in Vodafone "nobody thought he would go to prison", as though this now justified her actions. She used the pain of the Psychotic's parents as her get-out clause.

Chapter 28 Free speech. How to close down a website forum.

I started to publish details of the events of that year on a website very badly named fmicom.co.uk. It got quite a good number of hits from around the world, and lots from Vodafone. Mysteriously some time after Mr. Paul Wybrow left Vodafone to work in an associated company in Belgium.

Vodafone employed a top firm of solicitors, Herbert Smith, to close the site down. The site was hosted by BT (British Telecommunications).

BRITISH TELECOMMUNICATIONS PLC
Group legal Services
British telecommunications Centre
81 Newgate Street,
LondonECIA7AJ
For the attention of MS E GRACE

Dear Sirs
http://w\vw.fmicom.co.uk

Thank you for your letter of 2nd December 1999 and MP Stone's letter of 17th December 1999. As suggested in MP Stone's letter of 17th December 1999, the material about which our client complained during the latter part of 1999 has now re-appeared on the above website (together with some additional material). We remain of the view that the material contained on the website is defamatory of our client and that any such defamatory statements are actionable.
We would again refer you to the case of Godfrey -v- Demon Internet Limited (The Times, 27 March 1999) in which an internet service provider was held to have published a defamatory posting which was available through one of its newsgroups.
In the circumstances we would request that British Telecommunications Plc take whatever steps are appropriate to ensure that this defamatory material is no longer available via this website.
We look forward to hearing from you.

Yours faithfully

HERBERT SMITH

Exchange House
Primrose Street
London EC2A 2HS
Telephone +44 (0)20 7374 8000
Facsimile +44(0)2073740888
DX28
HERBERT SMITH
Bangkok Beijing Brussels Hong Kong London Moscow Paris Singapore
A list of the names of the partners and their professional qualifications is
open to inspection at the above office..

The eminent solicitors Herbert Smith used the device of Godfrey vs
Demon Internet to threaten BT with prosecution if they did not remove
my discussion site.

So I responded.

27th. September 1999
BT Webworld,
www.fmicom.co.uk

Further to my telephone calls on Saturday and this morning, I would
confirm that as soon as notification of the complaint was received, a new
index.htm was put on to the site, to inform that the site is now temporarily
suspended. I would also confirm that no further actions or updates will
occur to this site unless or until authority to do so is received from
BTWebworld.

As briefly discussed, all attempts over more than two years to resolve
some extremely important matters have failed.

I recently had a meeting with Mrs. Pauline Best, Director of Human
Resources, and Mrs. Natalie Fraser-King of Vodafone's legal
department, at which Mrs. Best requested a copy of my 'report', after
which she would consider an investigation.

On the website I have noted that Mrs. Best had already conducted an
'investigation' a year ago, confirmed apparently that the matters had
been accurately recorded, and that no further action was necessary.

At that last meeting, Mrs. Best did not know that the name of the person
with whom I attempted to discuss my initial report concerning, and with,
Mr. Paul K was Mrs. Alison Stanton. As I informed Mrs. Best, these
matters have never been in dispute, and I enclose example

correspondence. No replies have ever been received from Mrs. Alison Stanton to any of the relevant correspondence.

I have gone to very considerable lengths to establish the truth of those events without resorting to publication. This has included suggesting to Mr. Chris Gent that a meeting of all involved would resolve all of this within thirty minutes. As Mrs. Best is aware, the reasons for my actions include wishing to put the record straight concerning Mr. Paul K, and to ensure that people, particularly young people, do not ever enter anything like Vodafone's 'Business Systems' department.

When the website was first set up, it simply contained one letter to Mr. Paul Wybrow, and one to Mrs. Chris Gent, with an initial background. As you may see from the site, it was requested that Mr. Wybrow and Mr. Gent provide open and honest replies, whereupon the site would become redundant and Mr. Best could continue her investigation in private. Mr. Wybrow has for a very long time refused to answer these questions, and avoided any meeting.

I would be willing to provide copies of all correspondence to BT, and to meet with BTs legal department in conjunction with Vodafone, and then whoever wants to take legal action against me may then do so. I confirm that everything on the website is an accurate history of events, although views on structures and motivations are obviously my own.

In attempting to make fmicom.co.uk an open forum for discussion, I have informed Mrs. Best that I am willing to publish in full any documents from Vodafone's 'file' on me, and any other views or comments. As you may also see from a recent letter to Mrs. Alison Stanton, I have requested that she inform me of any errors of fact or interpretation, and any other information she considers relevant, and that I would publish all such communications unedited and in full.

If you would kindly inform me of any further information you require at this time, I will provide this as soon as possible.
Yours sincerely,
JN

I wrote to Mrs. Pauline Best :

Reading
Berkshire
6th. February 2000

Mrs Pauline Best
Vodafone Ltd.,
The Courtyard,
2-4 London Road,
Newbury,
Berkshire RG14 1JX

Dear Mrs. Best

I am in receipt of your letter of the 3rd. November 1999, which is both misleading and inaccurate. However, I have since been in communication with BT, and a way forward has been agreed. I have separated this communication into a number of sections for clarity.

The agreed way forward.

Existing documentation.

As soon as precise and accurate information is received from you with regard to web content you claim is false or defamatory, such content will be immediately removed with appropriate explanation.

Future documentation

All future website content will be provided to you in advance. If within seven days, no notification is received from you, the content will be published.

Vodafone contribution.

The website, and correspondence, has repeatedly confirmed that any information from Vodafone corporately, or from individuals, will be published in full and without any form of censorship.

Legal Action.

You have on a number of occasions in writing, and verbally, stated that should any information be published which is detrimental to Vodafone, 'you make take legal action'. You are now positively invited to take such action should you feel it appropriate. This will hopefully once and for all

126

achieve a resolution, involving as it will, Mr. Chris Gent, Mr. Paul K, and others. It may also prove to be of minor interest to the national and international press.

Communication.

Would you please provide an email address for all future communications. I would also be pleased if you would from now on address all communications to Issues@Vodafear.com (an alternative URL for the site.). This will allow effective communications between all involved, including BT.

Re : your letter of the 3rd. November 1999

Utmost

You state "The Company has done its utmost to address your concerns". The website will illustrate that the sentence should be changed to "The Company has done its utmost to ensure that none of these events are made public knowledge."

Unfortunately

You state "Unfortunately a solution was not reached.". The website will publish all correspondence with yourself and others, to which I trust you cannot possibly have any objection. You are requested to provide your reasons why, despite over two years, `a solution` was not reached.

Defamatory

`Defamatory material` -my understanding of the word, which may not be correct, is that for a statement to be defamatory it must be untrue. I have confirmed to BT that everything on the website is an accurate record of events, although views on motives and structures are of course my own.

Removed

You state `Now that it (the site) has been removed ...`. The site has never been removed. As soon as the initial notification was received, the site voluntarily put up a temporary index.htm awaiting clarification. I would be grateful if you did not persist with such misinformation. The site has been back to it`s original for some time, and agreement has been reached with BT as described in section 1 above.

No Action shall be taken by Vodafone.

May I suggest that instead of attempting to put unspecified pressure on BT, that you instead contribute to the site, or take appropriate legal action, as described in section 1 above.

I trust that this matter is now at an end.

This matter is only just beginning. Please see section 4 below.

Responses from Mr. Chris Gent and Mr. Paul Wybrow.

As you are fully aware, the site was only set up after two years of effort to keep the matter confidential. The site, when it was set up, requested only simple answers to simple questions from Mr. Paul Wybrow, whereupon your `investigation` could continue in private, and the site would be closed down. Mr. Wybrow has consistently refused to answer the simple questions, and avoided all meetings.

Your previous statement "I do not think that it is appropriate for a response at this time" (from Mr. Wybrow), might, to an impartial observer, suggest that both yourself and Mr. Wybrow consider the protection of Mr. Wybrow is of greater importance than the welfare of Mr. K`s family, my family, and others involved.

The future.

The first objectives of the website www.vodafear.com are included on it, and were openly agreed with you at our last meeting. None of those events occurred by accident or coincidence, and future publications will trace the causes from the first days of the organisation labelled `Vodafone`.

Summary

An agreed way forward has been determined with BT with regard to the website content, and I am sure must now be agreeable to yourself, to allow free and open examination of the issues, while ensuring full responsibility of all concerned.

Please forward all contributions (to Issues@vodafear.com) which will be fully published on the site.

If, despite the efforts of all involved, you still wish to suppress these matters, may I suggest that the honourable action would now be to immediately commence legal action against me.

I have forward copies of this letter to those concerned at BT, and have also written to Sir Peter Bonfield, Chief Executive of BT.

Yours sincerely

Jerry N

And a further letter to BT

Mr. Steven.J.Hewlett
Customer Services Manager
BT Connect To Business
Stadium House
pp618a 5 Park Street
CARDIFF South Glamorgan CF1 1NT

Dear Mr. Hewlett,

BT WebWorld - FmiCom.co.uk

Further to my recent telephone call, I enclose herewith a copy of my letter to Mrs. Pauline Best, Director of Human Resources at Vodafone, copied to Mr. Chris Gent.

No response has been received to this letter in the last fourteen days.

I am very much aware that BT are in a most difficult position with regard to the communications forum www.fmicom.co.uk,. However, I would like to re-confirm the following :

•   Every effort has been made to resolve these issues over the last two years, without resort to publication. 'Vodafone' have consistently avoided all such opportunities.

•   I have repeatedly emphasised that anything 'Vodafone' corporately, or individually, would wish to contribute to the forum, would be published completely and without any form of censorship.

•   If Vodafone consider anything on the website to be libellous, they have full recourse at law, and have at least a responsibility to identify and produce some initial evidence.

•   As previously stated, I confirm that everything on the website is an accurate record of events, although of course views on motivations and structures are subjective, and are my own.

•   The purpose of the website is to enable and encourage all contributions to understand why such events could have occurred, and to illustrate the causes, most particularly to young people.

I have no wish to involve BT in any dispute, and now do not see why they should become so. I would like to comment that individuals have, or should have, the same quality of consideration as 'corporations', with regard to the opportunities for freedom of responsible expression provided by the world-wide web.

I therefore intend to resume development of the forum immediately, and hope that I may have your understanding in this matter.

Yours sincerely,

JN

I wrote to Herbert Smith for details of what they considered `defamatory`. They did not reply. They did not need to. I did not of course get a reply from Mrs. Best of Vodafone.   The silence of their triumph.

BT had no choice, but had to close the site down. If they did not, they risked prosecution by Vodafone. I did however receive a communication which said "Sir Peter Bonfield (the Chairman of BT) has asked me to thank you for your letter of 14 November 1999 and enclosure. Your comments have been noted.

I wrote to the Office For The Supervision of Solicitors, to say surely Herbert Smith or Vodafone must have to identify what was apparently `defamatory`. But the Office For The Supervision of Solicitors did not act. I wrote to Robert Sayer, President of the Law Society, but he could not act. I wrote to Oftel, but they said they did not get involved in such matters.

Following this deceit, Mrs. Pauline Best wrote in triumph "The Company has done its utmost to address your concerns". Unfortunately a solution was not reached. ", and that the site was now closed. Sometime previously, Mr Chris Gent had written "I'm sure Mrs. Best is doing her utmost…"

One time, I was talking to a reporter from the Financial Times (at the time of the Mannesman affair) who was going to run the story. He came back to me and said "if Vodafone would threaten BT and individuals like you, think what they would do to a newspaper". His editor would not run the story. Ironically a few weeks later, there was an article in the same newspaper concerning the Mannesman takeover praising Vodafone. The article said "this will determine the future of Capitalism in Europe.

Some time later, I restarted the website with another Internet Provider and vodafear.com continued, and continues to this day. If we use it responsibly, the world-wide web may be the guardian of our freedom of speech.

Chapter 29 Home

The woman Mrs. Pauline Best who banned all communication, threatened legal action, and illegally closed a discussion website is now "Global People Development Director" of Vodafone. She was the author of the corporate description of their morals, entitled "Vodafone Values".

The woman Jane Boiston who phoned the Psychotic to warn him and got rid of the fine woman is now "Head of Organisational Development" at Vodafone.

The man who lied and deceived and to the question "Does Vodafone care anything about people?" sat silently grinning and shaking his head, is now Chief Technology Officer and Chief Information Office of Vodafone.

The man who wrote "I'm sure Mrs Best is doing her utmost.." and was unable to answer the simplest of questions became the Lifetime President of Vodafone.

It was their place, their home. The Psychotic said "I don't care what I do as long as I can work at Vodafone.

I was going to propose much more detailed analysis of the structures and motivations and morals but perhaps that can wait for another publication, and I'm sure you've had just about enough of this now.

I will produce a short supplementary publication on the matters of all such empires, of caste systems, of hierarchies of fear and obedience, of corporate empires of arrogance and labels of self-worth. All of this upon our beautiful, magical planet spinning in an unknowable universe. I have only ever envied one man, and that was the first man to land on the moon and look down upon the planet of his birth.

The next Chapter is the penultimate. May I just add one more paragraph to this.

Do you know what is the most ridiculous, hilarious sentence that was ever uttered by a man? It was uttered by me. Before Vodafone I had worked with the most beautiful people in a wonderful small company, but they had re-located to Scotland and I could not go with them. At my interview with Jane Boiston and the Psychotic I was asked "What is it you are looking for in Vodafone ? " I replied "This may seem silly, but what I'm looking for is a place that is so right, it's a home." Jane Boiston then uttered one sentence. It was a key to the Psychotic, but she did not know it.

Chapter 30   A convenient God

The Psychotic was not bad, was not evil, but was ill. There were a number of people who cared about him. Jo did, she went to great lengths to try and communicate with him. Fenella did, she tried to help him. Robert did, he just worked and worked to try and helped everybody including the Psychotic. Vanessa in her own way did, although it was disguised. I did for some time, but then became diseased with my own hatred, and at least I went to great lengths to keep all matters private.

Jane Boiston did not care about him. Alison Stanton did not care about him. Niall Garrett did not care about him. Paul Sayers did not care about him. The nasty little Paul Kerridge did not care about him. Nicki Hodgson did not care about him. And of course, the grinning and deceitful Paul Wybrow did not care about him, for he was concerned only with the protection of his own `career`

Paul Wybrow sat in the office and said "You're a caring person, you're a caring person" as though this fool knew anything about me, and as though it was a consolation prize.

On the 11th. March 1998 the Psychotic wrote to me from his prison cell. I am no better than the Psychotic, I have no more value. I have travelled the world with all of my own baggage, with my insecurities, with behaviour in my own forms of deviance from what is considered normal.

There is nothing new in anything I have written, all of these matters have been understood for thousands of years and in every part of our world. When I finally looked honestly at the I/me who has written this I remembered the Buddhist story of the man who had a magical stone with which he was able to see the true nature of people, and he would triumphantly expose their faults. It was only when he held the stone and inadvertently looked at his own reflection in the water that he was confronted with the horror of his own being.

This is what the Psychotic wrote :
Dear Jerry,

I received your letter yesterday and I was surprised to hear from you after so long. Nevertheless I am pleased that you have a job you are enjoying and only hope that it did not take you too long to find.

Since you ask, I am getting along fine in the circumstances. However I am not sure that going over past histories is of any benefit to anyone. What's gone has gone, Jerry, and nothing can change that. Lives change too ; friends, work colleagues, environments.. Even families don't seem to remain constant anymore.

Also while I would never deny anybody the right to an opinion, I do not feel that your conclusions on a "history of events" would be of much value to me, however well intended. Indeed you have done this in the past and I did not find it useful then. If I remember correctly it became rather personal if not derogatory in places, and with all due respect who are we to judge one another? There is only one who knows all and is qualified to judge.

As for people's feelings, these I agree are real enough, but whether these feelings are positive or negative will depend upon personal circumstances and experiences. Whilst I do not wish to seem dismissive or unfeeling towards others, I see little point in resurrecting the past.
For myself, like most people, I feel good and am grateful when feeling towards me are positive or compassionate. However when they are negative, I feel only sadness as certainly I feel myself part-responsible for engendering such a relationship which, after all, is two-way. I am truly sorry when relationships turn out this way, for never is there any ill-will or malice intended on my part. Maybe if you feel the circumstances are appropriate you might like to pass on the relevant part of this message for me.

In my last letter, several months ago, I did nothing to discourage you from keeping in touch, and indeed suggested that you might like to write. However it appears that you did not (write) and now there is nothing in your letter to give me any reason to feel we should keep in touch. After all there has never been anything other than a "work relationship" between us.

Circumstances put me in a position where I must "start again" as it were. I have the support of my family and some good friends, which is all I need for the time being. As I have suggested the past is gone and should remain just that. There really isn't any more to be said.

Finally if you are speaking to Jo again, please pass on my regards. I guess she must have had some really good memories from what must have been the trip of a lifetime. Also thank her for thinking of visiting me – it was a kind thought. I wish her all the best for the future, as indeed I do you too, Jerry. I'm just sorry that our relationship at Vodafone did not work out too well.

Best wishes Mr. K

Chapter 31 Mrs. Best's Vodafone Values

The Business Systems department of Vodafone did not own a Vodafone fone, because the V.A.T. authorities once questioned twenty-seven pence.

Paul Sayers controlled the Psychotic by increasing or decreasing his annual bonus. That year the value of the Psychotic's loss, that turned his rage to such an extreme, was about three pounds per week.

Once, in the Marketing Development office I saw an invoice for six hundred pounds for Vodafone umbrellas for a corporate event.

Christopher Gent, Lifetime President, "admitted that they had probably paid one billion pounds too much for the 3G licence in the U.K.". (A statement of such folly.)

Vodafone later wrote down billions and billions of electric money for overvalued assets.

John Tingey once caught a man out for forgetting to remove a sixty pence bottle of water from his expenses.

I had entered into this world on a cold day. I had entered a play that the actors had been playing long before I arrived. In the empire of fear obedience, hierarchies and labels of self-worth, they all saw the events of the Psychotic, all knew them, and as they danced their pre-determined steps in the same repeated patterns, they had no enterprise to change.

Near the end of the nineteenth century, in a small market town, a group of people came together to begin the development of a new concept which was `mobile telephony`. It would prove one of the greatest boom industries ever, until every human being in the word owned one. The purpose of mobile phones was that people could better communicate with each other. People need to communicate and enjoy communicating, because we are all one.

There were many ways in which these people could have come together. They could have come together as individuals who did not want to work or share with others, in which case they should have achieved nothing. They could have come together as communists, working together, from each according to his ability, to each according to his needs. They could have come together as a co-operative, each equal and sharing their skills and knowledge, and taking equally the rewards.

They could have come together as a nineteenth-century capitalist hierarchy of class and caste systems, where human beings were classified and valued according to the inherited rules of social control. They could have come together in an environment that evolved into an empire of fear, obedience and arrogance, where those who had no ability could exist as parasites and passengers. And with the pillars of share price and subscriber numbers, the illusion of authority and control and non-equality could flourish, right until the money ran out.

A man called Christopher Gent, a grey conformist, discovered that when the Empire threatened, others conceded. When you wanted to acquire something you could use your own currency, the share price that the Psychotic so often shouted. And for a few moments the expensive grey suit was accompanied by bright red braces of apparent boldness. This man understood nothing of the fundamentals of our monetary systems, that all representational forms of money as a store of value must eventually resolve themselves to the real work of humans or have no value. At one time, in a small market town, there were two men who worked in the collective labelled 'Vodafone'. One was the future 'Lifetime President', the other was the Psychotic. Both wore the same suit. One discovered that with corporate arrogance you could acquire anything and be accountable to no-one. The other discovered that if you understood the rules of the Empire, you would be protected and promoted and valued. How little the difference between the outcomes of our existence.

If I could work magic, I would glue back together all of the atoms of the human who was called Gerald Whent. And when I had glued back the billions of atoms I would give it life again, but not before I had burned all of these images into its brain. And when it announces it is a `benign dictator` all of our children may see the truth. I would give it everlasting life, so that it would no longer have the greatest fear of all, the fear of it's own mortality. Vodafear.

BACentre Publications
Division of Business Analysis Centre Ltd,
Reading, UK